TRIUMPH

Inspiring True Stories of
Challenge and Spiritual Growth

Edited By
Nechemia Coopersmith
Shraga Simmons

aish.com
A Targum Press Book

First published 2006
Copyright © 2006 by Aish.com
ISBN 1-56871-411-4

Published by:
TARGUM PRESS, INC.
22700 W. Eleven Mile Rd.
Southfield, MI 48034
E-mail: targum@targum.com
Fax: 888-298-9992
www.targum.com

Distributed by:
FELDHEIM PUBLISHERS
208 Airport Executive Park
Nanuet, NY 10954

Printing plates by Frank, Jerusalem
Printed in Israel by Chish

לזכר נשמת

LAWRENCE HYTMAN ז״ל

אריה לייב בן אברהם ז״ל

A man of true חסד who personified
the words: ואהבת לרעך כמוך

To mark his 15th yahrtzeit
י״ט אלול תשנ״א

By his
children and grandchildren

CONTENTS

ACKNOWLEDGMENTS

Our endless gratitude goes to the talented team at Aish.com: David LeVine, Jack Kalla, Yitzhak Attias, Seth Aronstam, Benyamin Buxbaum, Chavi Kahanowitz, Leba Jacobowitz, Shoshana Goldberg, Tamara Yogev, Esther Emanuel, Chaya Richmond, Mike Cooper, Rabbi Pinchas Waldman, Rabbi Mordechai Younger and Rabbi Kalman Packouz. Your dedication and expertise are the fuel that drives the Aish.com engine.

To Rabbi Noah Weinberg, founder and dean of Aish HaTorah, whose wisdom and inspiration is the guiding light for all that we do.

To all the supporters of Aish.com, for their generous financial assistance and invaluable guidance. In particular we thank Yuri and Deana Pikover, Sharon and Jonathan Faith, Mitch and Joleen Julis,

Art and Sally Klein, Bob and Michelle Diener, Dov and Nancy Friedberg, Andrea and Stuart Hytman, and Dennis Berman, for their tremendous support and dedication.

To the excellent staff at Targum Press.

To all the Aish.com writers, whose inspiring content made this book possible. It is an honor to work with you.

To the hundreds of thousands of loyal and dedicated readers — your feedback, enthusiasm and support has been instrumental in making Aish.com the leading Jewish educational website.

To our wives, who believe in the power of Aish.com to nudge the world, one small click at a time, in a more positive direction.

And to the Almighty, who grants us the privilege of sharing His infinite wisdom and makes miracles happen every day.

Nechemia Coopersmith and Shraga Simmons
Jerusalem, November 2006 / Cheshvan 5767

DR. JACKIE YARIS

PEANUT BUTTER TIME

I t was one of those mornings. I was up all night on call and exhausted. It was dark and rainy outside, and my three kids woke up late without any recollection that getting dressed is a daily ritual. All I wanted to do was go back to bed, but instead I went through their rooms and chirped, "Wake up, sleepyheads. It's a school day, time to get dressed..." with a fake smile and forced cheerfulness.

No one was interested.

"Come on, sillies," I continued in a singsong voice through clenched teeth, "it's time to get dressed."

Dr. Jackie Yaris is a physician practicing internal medicine in Beverly Hills, CA. She is also a wife and the mother of three young children.

After 15 minutes of escalating "reminders," my voice had become oddly falsetto, my oldest son Josh was dueling on his Gameboy, my middle son Joey was using the time to rearrange his furniture, and my little angel Julia was color-coordinating her shoes.

No one was the slightest bit ready. Ten minutes later, I could feel my heart palpitating in my ears, and I was pinching my palm to keep from screaming. Thankfully, my husband heard the hysteria that tinged my voice and came to take over. As I walked downstairs I stumbled on a cup of milk left from the night before and gritted my teeth as I watched tiny rivulets of milk drip from one step to the next. Though I had tried deep, controlled breathing, my internal growl was becoming audible.

Joey came down first, red hair sticking straight up and shirt on backwards.

"What do you want for breakfast?" I managed.

Perhaps calling to mind what would be the pinnacle of breakfast experiences, he said dreamily, "I think I'll have marshmallows and yellow M&Ms..." Seeing the wild look in my eyes, he quickly reconsidered. "How about cereal?"

"Better choice," I hissed.

Next, Josh launched his backpack down the banister and I cringed as it landed with a thud and scattered.

Just then Julia, whose pouty lips and dainty features belie her inner strength and persistence, pounded down the stairs wearing her annoying sparkly shoes that with each step discharged red glitter that congealed with the milk mess. She was chanting, "I want peanut butter! I want peanut butter!" The deep breathing didn't work. There was just something about that high-pitched peanut butter whine that did it.

I inhaled one last time, and in my loudest voice, punctuating every word, I bellowed, "It Is Not Peanut Butter Time!!!"

The house went silent. I heard a muffled giggle. Everyone stared at me. My husband was smart enough not to verbalize the question that played across his face.

I don't know if peanut butter has a time, or when exactly that might be, but I did know I'd had enough.

Though I continued my breathing and tried to relax, an hour later my head was still spinning when I went to work.

On my desk was a patient's chart I needed to review. Though I hadn't seen Mrs. Mesa for over two years, I remembered her from my file. She was then around 50, slightly overweight, and worked at a sedentary desk job. She joked that her cholesterol might be a bit high because she had just returned from an Alaskan cruise to celebrate her 30th wedding anniversary. I remember how her warm, brown eyes sparkled when she said the extra cholesterol would be worth all the good food.

I was shocked when I got her labs back the next day. It wasn't her cholesterol that was high, but her liver tests — elevated to critical levels, over five times normal. As I looked at the results I felt like an interloper to a cascading of fates that had already begun in her body.

I remember trying to sound nonchalant when I called to tell her we needed to repeat the labs. But I could tell by her halting, pinched questions that she understood that somewhere, in the space of one conversation, the prism had shifted. The straight controlled edges of her "healthy" existence had shattered and contorted into the terrifying uncontrolled shards of illness.

The abnormal labs led to an ultrasound, which led to a biopsy, which led to a diagnosis of hepatitis C, which led to liver failure. And now, two years later, I was sending this chart with its description of a joyous 54-year-old mother of three across town to a premier transplant center, where she waited, in end-stage liver failure, for a precious liver. End-stage liver patients all look eerily similar — bloated, bald and greenish yellow. I shuddered when I tried to imagine her that way, and hoped that the sparkle of her brown eyes was able to transcend their sickly amber background.

What haunted me, though, was the fact that the hepatitis C had been lurking, undiagnosed for over 20 years since a blood transfusion during the delivery of her third child. I kept wondering: If she had known that a virus was methodically insinuating its deadly genetics into the cells of her liver, would she have lived her life differently?

Would she have stopped even if she were in the middle of making dinner to go outside and revel in the watercolor palate that is a winter sunset? Or if she happened to see a spiderweb after a rainfall, would she have noticed that it becomes a crystalline lattice-work in the fledgling sunlight? Or, after a frantic, screamy morning rushing her kids to school, would she have looked beyond the chaos and inhaled the sweet musty glow of their laughter and excitement?

It was only then that I noticed the jagged palpitations of my own frantic, screamy morning had receded.

I was thinking about that when I went to the waiting room to call in my new patient — Elaine, a 28-year-old. I was struck by her elegance as she slowly stood, threw back her head and glided toward me — her long brown hair, dark skin and green eyes gave her an unusual, exotic look. She had flirted with the elderly people sitting there, and they appreciatively smiled and stared as she walked toward me. She was stunning, but something about her was haggard.

Elaine worked on Rodeo Drive selling ridiculously expensive clothing to ridiculously rich people, but like many newcomers to L.A., she was hoping to be "discovered." She slumped into my office chair and shook her head wearily. "This city is wearing me down... I'm sure that's why I'm so tired all the time... I'm just so tired."

I was surprised by the innocence and sincerity in her Midwestern twang. "It's so hard, being this far from my family...they're in Nebraska...especially my mom. She really needs me since Dad died. I have two older brothers, but I'm her only daughter."

I glanced up to see the wide peanut butter grin of my own daughter beaming brightly from a frame on my desk.

"My mom made me come, she's so worried. I've been bloated and constipated for about a month. I'm sure it's nothing, but you know how moms are."

Constipation is extremely common, but any change in bowel habit warrants further exploration, so I ordered an ultrasound and talked to her about dietary changes.

I didn't think about it again until about 8 p.m., when a radiologist paged me. The ultrasound showed a mass, he said. He wasn't sure if it was ovarian or colon, but she certainly needed a follow-up CT scan. And the cascade had begun.

I shut my eyes and took a deep breath. I was shocked. I knew the possibilities, and none were good: Ovarian cancer? Colon cancer? Lymphoma? Though it was late and I was exhausted, I couldn't sleep. I was plagued by the phone call I would have to make to Elaine the next day.

I knew as soon as I would begin to speak, her wistful eyes would blur with terror as she, too, would be forced to look through the prism of the sick. But from experience, I also knew that eventually her eyes would again focus, and it would be on an entirely different reality. Though a diagnosis brings a terrifying disorientation, it also yields a striking clarity. Somehow it cuts through the haze of the trivial and the fog of petty concerns, and what emerges is pure and real.

What I couldn't understand was why does it take a diagnosis to see clearly? I lay awake a long time thinking about that.

The next morning no magic had happened. The kids woke up late and still did not want to get dressed. Joey was busy moving his furniture, Josh was intently beating a bad guy on his Gameboy and Julia was now color-coordinating her dresses. And I stood back and watched, as if through a prism.

Nothing was different, but everything had changed.

Eventually, everyone came down dressed, and only a few minutes late. This time though, when I saw Josh's untucked shirt, what I really noticed was his mischievous glint that contained a joyful exuberance as he bounded down the stairs, two at a time. And Joey, with red hair mussed, practically glowed as he proudly beamed, "Mama, I moved *all* my furniture!" And when Julia rambled down the stairs, the airborne red glitter caught the sun and sparked to the ground like firework tails.

When she asked for peanut butter this time, I thought about my patient's mother, alone and so far away, and how lucky I was that I could still enfold my daughter in my arms and all she needed was a little peanut butter. I nodded and she squealed, "It's peanut butter time! It's peanut butter time!"

And on that musty, sweet, peanut butter-scented morning, I rejoiced.

RABBI YAAKOV SALOMON

TRAVELS WITH MY EGO

I wrote a book.

I wish I could say that it doesn't matter to me if you buy it, read it or like it. But I'd be lying. It *does* matter to me. A lot.

Am I proud that I feel that way? No. Does it mean that I am insecure, vulnerable and on wobbly terrain? No. It means I am normal (at least in this area of life). All of us, to varying degrees, are concerned with the

Rabbi Yaakov Salomon, C.S.W. is a noted psychotherapist, in private practice in Brooklyn, NY for over 25 years. He is a senior lecturer and the creative director of Aish HaTorah's Discovery Productions. He is also an editor and author for the ArtScroll Publishing Series, and a featured writer on Aish.com. Rabbi Salomon shares his life with his wife, Temmy, and their unpredictable family.

opinions that others have of us, especially when we display and disclose our feelings, skills, beliefs, activities and idiosyncrasies to the public eye. That's how we are wired.

And so, my ego and I were trekking down Coney Island Avenue some weeks ago, when we chanced past Berman's, one of the local Judaica Bookshops. This was not an uncommon occurrence. My ego and I often travel together, as we do share assorted common interests and pursuits.

I was not surprised, therefore, when he turned to me and said:

Lots of books in Berman's window, but where is yours?

Predictably, I gulped. It was not the first time I had noticed the glaring omission in the window. But, for some reason, this time I decided to venture inside. *Maybe (gasp) they don't even SELL my book!* I had to find out.

I meandered my way past the CDs, the ArtScroll Talmud volumes and some genuine customers, and parked myself at the "New Releases" section. There were several copies of my book. Relieved, I lifted one of them and tried very hard to appear like an ordinary book browser. Secretly, I hoped that others might notice, take the hint and also peek at my book. They didn't. But I didn't stop there.

"This is my book," I offered to the young sales clerk. "How's it selling?"

"Okay, I guess... I don't really know," he replied without looking up.

I didn't stop there.

"I know this sounds a little funny," I stammered, "but my kids are always asking me why my book is not in the window."

It felt kind of pathetic. Here I was, a grown man, practically begging to see my book in the window. But, it worked.

"No problem," he answered. "Go ahead...slip one in."

I did.

Ten seconds later I was back on the sidewalk, reunited with my ego, and proudly peering at the newly adorned window. Frankly, it looked good. In fact, the whole display somehow seemed brightened by the new addition (yeah right). I smiled too broadly and scampered home.

Fast forward a few days. I'm on my way to the drugstore for a Diet Snapple. And as I walk past Berman's, my eyes automatically dart to the right for a quick and proud glance at my book in the window. Only one problem — it isn't there. It's gone!

My book had been replaced by...by...some *other* book, the name of which I forgot instantly. I stood there in mortal silence, pretending that it didn't matter and wondering what to do next. I felt like I had been duped. The clerk who had instructed me to put the book in the window had, in fact, only been humoring this pitiable and desperate soul, but as soon I left the scene he promptly removed it and restored it to its rightful place — buried on a lonely, dusty shelf.

I continued my journey to the drugstore, but my pace had now slowed considerably and my shoulders probably dropped an inch or two as well. I wasn't sure what I was more upset about — the book having been removed, or the fact that it bothered me. Either way, I wasn't a pretty sight.

Arriving at the store, I headed straight for the refrigerator. I half-expected them to be out of my favorite flavor, but I was wrong. I snatched the bottle off the shelf and trudged over to the check-out counter. The girl behind the register was unfamiliar to me. She rang up my Snapple and counted some change. This simple transaction was about to end. But then she looked at me, and with just a few words, she transformed my paltry purchase into a mood-altering event.

"*What the Angel Taught You*, right?" she said.

She had uttered the title of a previous book I had written and recognized me as the author. I tried to stop my grin, but it was of no use.

"Why...er...yes. How did you know?"

"Oh, I've heard you speak many times, and I always watch your weekly video blog on Aish.com. It's wonderful. Besides, I've read your book seven times! You're my favorite author."

If the Snapple hadn't been on the counter, it would have skidded out of my hand into a thousand shards on the floor. There wasn't much I could say. I just stood there, dumbfounded, with the stupid grin growing wider and me probably straightening my tie or something.

I thanked her a bit more than I should have and told her about my *new* book. She seemed excited and promised to pick one up right away. Collecting my drink, I awkwardly marched to the exit. Like a yo-yo on steroids, my psyche had just been pummeled and exalted, beaten and hoisted, crushed and invigorated. And all within a few seconds.

It reminded me of the credo of a great chassidic leader. I believe it was Reb Mendel of Kotsk. It was said that he lived his life according to two major philosophies. One was the declaration by Abraham of supreme humility, when he prayed to God for the welfare of the people of Sodom, "For I am but dust and ash" (Genesis 18:27). The second was the dictum of our Sages of the Talmud of ultimate responsibility, "It is incumbent upon everyone to say, 'The entire world was created just for me' " (Sanhedrin 37a).

Those closest to him say that he wrote each passage on a separate piece of paper, and that he kept both papers with him at all times, in separate pockets.

"The complexities of living require the implementation of both schools of thought," he would teach. "Sometimes we must feel like we are so very small; other times we must realize that the entire universe revolves around each of us. The secret of life is to know when to reach into which pocket."

The events of that day had thrown me from one end of the emotional spectrum to the other, but *both* of those reactions were ego-driven. I had allowed the perceptions of others to completely dictate my equilibrium. I was just a frail reed, blowing in a gust of vanity.

Contrast that insecurity with the sanguine mentality of the rebbe. He taught that it is our inner choices that should dictate how we feel, not external opinions. There are times we should focus on the inherent, objective greatness that resides in each and every soul, feeling empowered to put our unique stamp on the world. And there are times we should have the humility to sense our inherent smallness.

These emotions can never emerge from the reactions of those around us. We must not allow ourselves to be overwhelmed by rejection or intoxicated by the limelight.

Instead, when we feel small, it is a healthy realization that without a Supreme Being we can accomplish nothing. And when we feel big, it is because our potential for change and growth is truly endless.

Tell that to your ego, next time you travel together.

DEBBIE HIRSCHMANN

OUT OF THE CLOSET

Okay, I'll admit it. I'm a closet Jew.

You'd probably never know that I'm Jewish. I have blond hair and green eyes. I don't wear a Star of David — never would — that's what they had to wear in Nazi Germany. I really don't talk about Judaism to people outside of my community. I really don't make it public that I'm a Jew, and particularly don't disclose that I'm a religious Jew. So I live in the closet as a Jew. And until recently, I preferred it that way.

There are many reasons for my secrecy. But I realize now, they're mostly because of the Holocaust.

Debbie Hirschmann has a degree from UCLA in physiological sciences and a master's in business from USC. She previously worked in the pharmaceutical industry and lives in the Los Angeles Aish community with her husband and two daughters.

My mother and her sister are Holocaust survivors, and their parents were murdered in the gas chambers at Auschwitz. When my mom speaks of her parents, she still always cries, heartbroken, as if it just happened yesterday. As if she were still that teenager whose parents were ripped out of her life, forever.

I always had very mixed feelings about the Holocaust. On one hand, I was powerfully drawn to it and wanted to know more about it. On the other hand, it caused Judaism to have such a horrible stigma. As a result, all things Jewish had a negative association that I didn't want to have anything to do with. I didn't want to be associated with the persecuted Jew. So I pushed both the Holocaust, and Judaism, away.

To add to all this, I was hardly raised Jewish at all. My mother married a Catholic, and so I was raised with really no religion of which to speak. My mother always said, "Hitler was our matchmaker." In other words, had her family been alive, she never would have married a non-Jew. My parents agreed not to push either of their religions on my sister or me, and they kept with that agreement.

In my WASPy public high school in suburban San Francisco, I never admitted to anyone why I missed school on the Jewish New Year. I certainly wasn't Bat Mitzvahed; it never crossed my mind. We went to temple just two days a year, Rosh Hashana and Yom Kippur. In temple I recall my mother and her sister crying, or sitting with pained looks on their faces. No spiritual meaning for me, just more negativity. Every year, on schedule, I sat watching my mother and aunt, who had suffered so much already, suffer yet again.

We celebrated both Christmas and Chanukah, but I always felt that Chanukah was a poor substitute for the Christmas that we celebrated with joy and beauty. I always felt sorry for my cousins who only celebrated Chanukah, with its dismal decorations. In our home, next to a beautifully decorated Christmas tree, pathetically sat a tarnished, copper menorah with unattractive wax candles. To "celebrate" Chanukah, my mother always cried and sang a song in Hebrew that her father sang when he was alive.

As I got older, I searched for God and meaning in this world, but didn't get answers through religion. Since no Jewish education was available, I explored being a born-again Christian. I got into it for a while, but could never really buy into the idea of needing a middleman. The last straw came when I was at a Bible study class. I asked how they knew what Jesus exactly said and meant, since there had been so many translations and versions of the New Testament. They didn't like my question and basically said I should shut up and just have faith and not ask questions. At that point I threw in the towel with Christianity. Can't ask questions? Can't get answers? What kind of a religion is that? Blind faith wasn't my bag.

But neither was Judaism. Yet.

By sheer coincidence (a.k.a. God's will) I stumbled into traditional Judaism through Aish HaTorah with my soon-to-be husband. Slowly, we made the trek of becoming religiously observant — first going to a few Shabbats, then taking on more. I learned the incredible beauty of Judaism. I found that every one of my questions had a multitude of answers through Judaism. I felt that Judaism was — tragically! — an amazing, well-kept secret. Everything about it rang true.

I started learning and knowing about the religion that my grandparents had died for.

But still I was a closet Jew.

I still didn't want to be singled out as my family had been. *Der Juden!* As my mother always said, "You can be a Jew on the inside, but not on the outside." It was too risky to be a Jew on the outside.

But push finally came to shove, and although I didn't know it, this year I was about to get shoved out of my closet.

Work was now conflicting with Shabbat. The daylight savings time change was about to occur, and I was no longer comfortable with the idea that I might miss candlelighting on a Friday night because of a work commitment.

But what would they think of me? I can't expect to leave early just because I'm Jewish! Here I was, feeling that being Jewish was bad again.

But I knew I had to speak up.

Everyone has his or her tests. One of mine is work. I obsess over it, agonize over it, ruminate over it. My husband said, "You should be as afraid of God as you are of your boss." He was right. I had to get my priorities straight.

This last Rosh Hashana I prayed that I could put work into perspective. God answered my prayers. I knew that I had to tell my boss that I'm a religious Jew and I need to observe the laws of my religion.

I was incredibly uncomfortable with this idea. How could I say this to my boss? How would he respond?

I realized, in thinking what I would tell my boss, that I have two main reasons for being a religious Jew. One is because it gives enormous meaning, purpose and beauty to my life.

The other is that it finally let me come to terms with my relationship to the Holocaust. If I can practice Judaism, the same Judaism that the Nazis wanted to wipe from this earth, then my grandparents' deaths, and those of 6 million innocent Jews, would not be in vain. I am carrying on that which they died for. The Nazis did not win. Those innocents did not die in vain. Judaism lives on with me.

If people in concentration camps risked death to practice their religion, if starving Jews in concentration camps forfeited food to observe Yom Kippur, then certainly an extra hour of work on Friday was a sacrifice I could make.

When I picked up the phone to my boss, I asked God for the words. I started to explain my carefully prepared statement. I prefaced that this was a difficult discussion for me to have, because it's very personal, because it's very important to me, because... I'm Jewish. And I'm uncomfortable bringing this up because of my history, because being Jewish has never been seen as a very positive thing — that my mom had been in a concentration camp just because she was a Jew, and my grandparents were murdered just because they were Jewish. And then I burst into tears.

I burst into tears, for them, and also for me.

The phone call went swimmingly, and my boss was very accommodating. (I guess it's hard to say no to a woman bawling at the other end of the line.) And that week was such a relief when I didn't feel the need to go into hiding when Shabbat candlelighting came.

Finally accepting who I am.

Finally out of the closet.

SARA YOHEVED RIGLER

THIS IS A TEST

My friend Tzippy owned an antique diamond ring that had belonged to her grandmother. The ring was Tzippy's only family heirloom. When she washed her hands, she sometimes put the ring next to the soap dish in the bathroom.

One day Tzippy's husband David flushed the toilet and reached for the soap. As he did so, he saw a small, shiny object fly in an arc directly into the flushing toilet. He hurriedly found Tzippy in the

Sara Yocheved Rigler is a graduate of Brandeis University. Her spiritual journey took her to India and through 15 years of teaching Vedanta philosophy and meditation. Since 1985, she has been practicing Torah Judaism. She is a featured writer on Aish.com, and resides in the Old City of Jerusalem with her husband and children. She is the author of the acclaimed biography and spiritual manual, Holy Woman.

kitchen and asked her if she had left her ring by the soap dish. Tzippy glanced down at her finger and answered, "I suppose I did. Why?"

"Because I just flushed it down the toilet," was David's alarming answer.

Tzippy felt like screaming, "You what? That was my grandmother's ring! It's irreplaceable! How could you be so careless?!!"

Instead, she stopped herself. If she had lost her heirloom ring, she thought, why should she also lose her marital harmony? In soft, measured tones she asked, "Okay, so what should we do now?"

David, feeling dreadfully guilty, had been ready to defend himself against his wife's attack with a self-righteous counterattack: "How can you be so careless as to leave your valuable ring in a place like that?!" Since Tzippy did not attack, however, he answered humbly, "I'm really sorry. I guess we should call the plumber and ask him to check inside the pipes, but it's a real long shot."

Tzippy suggested that before they called the plumber, they should take a look in the bathroom. Perhaps the ring had fallen next to the toilet, not into it.

"I saw it fly into the flushing toilet," David insisted, but he went with her to satisfy her doubts.

They looked on the floor around the toilet and found nothing. Then they looked into the toilet bowl and could not believe their eyes. The ring was sitting there on a narrow porcelain shelf two inches above the bottom of the bowl.

"If I had screamed at my husband or he had screamed at me," Tzippy told me at the conclusion of her story, "I know the ring wouldn't have been there."

The concept of God testing human beings is as old as Judaism itself. According to the Midrash, God tested the patriarch Abraham 10 times, each test more difficult than the one before. The ultimate test was God's command to Abraham to sacrifice his beloved son Isaac. The Torah explicitly introduces this account with the words, "God tested Abraham" (Genesis 22:1).

What is the purpose of a divinely ordained test? A student is tested in school so that the teacher can find out how much the student knows. The omniscient God, by contrast, is already aware of a person's capacity before the test. The purpose of a Divine test, therefore, cannot be to reveal any new information to God.

The Midrash points out that the Hebrew word for "test," *nisah*, is derived from the word *nes*, meaning flag. As a flag flies high above and identifies an army or ship, so a test is meant to elevate and reveal the innate potential of the person being tested.

A test is always a choice at the upper limit of a person's capacity. Passing the test actually changes the person. Potential becomes actualized. A rose bud contains all the petals of the opened rose, but a rose in full bloom is far more beautiful than a bud. Abraham standing with a knife in his hand on Mount Moriah was a greater Abraham than he had been at the foot of the mountain.

Tests come in many disguises: someone else's ineptitude, a traffic jam, an unexpected (and unwanted) guest, a computer malfunction, a telephone call just as you're falling asleep, a financial loss, a child throwing a tantrum, a gratuitous insult, suggestions from your mother (or better yet, your mother-in-law) on how to raise your children, etc.

God doesn't give us a test we cannot pass. When we fail our tests, it's usually because we didn't recognize the situation as a test in the first place.

If only we could see a neon sign flashing in front of our mind's eye — "This is a test!" — all of us could muster enough patience, forgiveness, kindness, self-discipline, calmness, or whatever other character trait is called for, to pass the test. How tragically often it is only afterwards that we realize the test beneath the disguise, as we hit our foreheads in frustration and regret at a squandered opportunity to outgrow our limitations.

The key to recognizing a test is to remember that everything, *everything*, *EVERYTHING*, comes from God. God is the ultimate source of every occurrence, every financial loss, every traffic jam, every tantrum. Although humans have free will to choose between good and evil, what happens to any individual is determined by God. A thief can choose to mug a passerby on the corner of 23rd and Broadway at 2 a.m., just as you're on your way there, but if it isn't God's will for you to be mugged, you'll be delayed a block away, a policeman will show up just at that

33

moment, or the thief will run into an old pal who owes him money. That your 2-year-old throws his tantrum in the middle of an upscale department store surrounded by well-dressed singles shaking their heads and clicking their tongues is a deliberately scheduled Divine test for you.

So how can we recognize a test before we've blown it? Much of Jewish practice is geared toward recognizing God as the ultimate source, 24/7. Cultivating such God-consciousness puts us in the optimum mental posture to field a test when it comes, just as a well-seasoned tennis player assumes the perfect stance, ready to hit the ball before it comes flying over the net.

Saying blessings that acknowledge God as the source — before eating food and drinking, seeing the ocean or hearing thunder — is a sure-fire practice to sustain God-consciousness when the test comes flying at us. Twice-a-day recitation of the Shema, the affirmation that the transcendent God is also the Director of nature from moment to moment, is a better test-prep than crib notes.

My favorite method for remembering Reality when I'm about to "lose it" is to recite the first line of a laminated prayer I keep handy: "I believe with a firm belief that this trouble and distress that I am undergoing is ordained by Divine Providence, and I accept it upon myself with love." Remembering that the computer crash, the late-night phone call, or the gratuitous insult comes from God, Who loves me, does not render the bitter test suddenly sweet, but it could give me the right mindset to swallow the bitter medicine rather than spitting it out.

In the above story, Tzippy perceived that the ring was still there, in seeming defiance of the laws of physics, as a Divine reward for her husband and her passing their test. But surely God does not reward humans in the same way that a parent rewards a child who brings home a good grade.

Rewards for tests are similar to prayers fulfilled. When God grants our prayer, it's not because we have succeeded in convincing the Almighty to give us what we want. Rather, earnest prayer transforms us and makes us into bigger vessels, able to contain the blessings that God is always eager to bestow on us. Similarly, tests passed make us into bigger vessels, more able to contain even "supernatural" levels of Divine beneficence. Because Tzippy went beyond her nature and didn't yell, God's response was also "beyond nature."

A couple years ago, my family was vacationing on the Golan Heights, near the Sea of Galilee. One day we found an isolated beach, pulled our car over, and went swimming. In the water, my husband commented that he was nervous about losing the car key, which he had put into the pocket of his bathing suit.

"Are you kidding?" I upbraided him. "Your pocket is no place for the car key. Give it to me." I had zippered pockets and safely inserted the key.

The next day, we did a hike through one of the streams that feeds into the Sea of Galilee. This hike, popular in the heat of the Israeli summer, involves walking in waist-high water past lush, overhanging vegetation. At intervals, the stream forms delicious pools, where the hiker can dunk down and cool himself.

I was walking ahead with one of our children. Suddenly my husband, pale and distraught, caught up with us and announced, "I lost the car key. It must have happened when I dunked down a ways back."

"Where did you have it?" I asked, horrified.

"In my bathing suit pocket," he replied simply, as if I hadn't, just the day before, warned him about putting the key in his shallow pocket.

"Well, let's go back and look for it," I suggested with dawning desperation.

"No, we'll never find it in the mud, and I don't even remember exactly where I dunked."

I stood there staring at him, my mind quickly calculating the ramifications of his carelessness. My set of car keys was in my purse, locked inside the car. To open the car, we'd need to call a locksmith from Tiberias, but the cell phone was also locked inside the car. And even if a fellow hiker lent us a cell phone, how would we find a locksmith? How much would he charge to come all the way out here into the wilderness? How many hours would we have to wait?

I felt like screaming, "How could you?!" Then I remembered Tzippy and her ring. I knew, in a flash of clarity, that I was being tested. And I hoped that if I passed the test, perhaps God would get us out of this mess. So I flashed my husband a reassuring smile and said, "Let's just enjoy the rest of the hike. When we get back to the car, maybe one of the other hikers will know how to break into the car."

An hour later, we emerged from the stream onto the bank. Two trails led back to the parking lot. Our chosen trail led us through a Eucalyptus grove where a group had been making a barbeque. I saw people bidding each other goodbye and driving off in their cars. One vehicle, a Renault, caught my attention. The back doors were open to reveal some kind of technical equipment, but I couldn't make out what kind. *Perhaps*, I thought, *he has a tool we can use to pry the car door open.*

As I approached, I saw that the car's hood was up and a man was working on the engine. His wife was standing beside the vehicle. In my best Hebrew, I tried to explain to her what had happened, and asked her if her husband had any tools that could help us.

She replied that their car wouldn't start, so her husband had been trying to fix it for the last half hour. When he finished, she would ask him to help us.

No more than three minutes passed when I heard the sound of the engine turning over and purring. The wife apprised her husband of our plight. He came to where I was standing at the rear of the vehicle. I repeated my request, that perhaps he had some kind of tool to pry open the car door. He looked at me as if I were crazy, exclaimed something in Hebrew, and slammed one of the rear doors shut, revealing a sign that read: "Uri Locksmith."

Two minutes later, he was at our car. We watched with fascination as he deftly used his state-of-the-art tools to open the car door. As he walked away, he called over his shoulder: "You folks sure are lucky. If my car hadn't broken down, I'd have been gone from here half an hour ago."

Thank you, Uri. And thank you, Tzippy. And thank you, God!

DIANE FABER VEITZER
MY AFRICAN VACATION

My vacations are usually escapes to places where cares are few and comforts are many. This year I went where cares are many and comforts are few.

I took a trip with an organization that sends volunteers to developing nations to help with the daily tasks facing poor and hungry people struggling for a better life. Far from politics, boardrooms or budgets, volunteers lend a hand in simple activities such as keeping records in a medical clinic, assisting with construction of school buildings or teaching English conversation to children — tasks that require no

Diane Faber Veitzer writes from Los Angeles, CA.

special skills, just a little patience and some good humor.

I chose Ghana, the original starting place for the United States Peace Corps, where 50 years of democracy make it the jewel of West Africa, with no ongoing violence and a welcoming attitude toward outsiders who so rarely visit this corner of the world.

It is neither inexpensive nor easy to travel to West Africa. You cannot even enter Ghana without a certificate confirming a yellow fever immunization; my own doctor insisted on updates of tetanus, polio, typhoid and hepatitis A as well — hundreds of dollars of vaccines, none covered by ordinary insurance. I also took malaria pills, choosing between the weekly dose, which is known to cause paranoia, and the daily pill, which is much easier to forget and be rendered ineffective. Malaria is the number one cause of death in Ghana but one doctor warned a fellow volunteer that rabies is so rampant that if you are so much as scratched by a cat, your vacation is over immediately and you must airlift out of Africa for competent treatment. With my pack full of mosquito netting, a small pharmacy of drugs and remedies, and enough protein for three weeks, I set out on the long flight from Los Angeles to Ghana.

On my first full day in the capital city of Accra, I walked for hours through the national museum, the open market and residential areas. The next day, I joined my group of volunteers, and we took a bus to the coastal town where we would pass the next few weeks together as the only Caucasians for many miles.

Although our group accommodations were nicer than any of the local residents', they were still a far cry from any "hotel" most people would consider. No hot water, ever; intermittent electricity; lizards everywhere; and baby kittens about whom we warned each other by shouting "death kitty" in the dark.

The table in my room became the "staging area" for the beginning of each day. There, after climbing out from under my mosquito net in the morning, an array of malaria pills, mosquito repellant, antibacterial scrub, spring water, sunscreen, jungle hat and other preventatives greeted me as a sobering reminder that danger to life and health was ever-present. Ironically, traveling to the poorest country I'd ever visited became the most expensive vacation I'd ever taken!

My private stash of water, tuna, protein bars, multivitamins, Cipro, Zithromax, Sudafed, Tylenol, matzah and even more water formed a further protective barrier between the natural environment and me. In Ghana, the simple act of running one's toothbrush under the faucet would render it forever unusable.

Thus girded for battle against the elements, and aware of the dangers, I walked outside the hotel walls toward the elementary school where I was to work as an English teacher for two weeks. Goats mingled freely among young, barefoot children, both avoiding the open sewers that line the road on either side. Schools close when it rains, as muddy ground could lead to children sliding into the sewer trenches. Women stride, heads held high, balancing huge bowls of food or consumer goods on their heads, babies strapped on their backs. Rudimentary construction moves forward intermittently along the road, as need competes with cost to keep the projects going, but slowly.

On the first day, I was filled with trepidation wondering how the local people would react to these outsiders appearing in their streets. I needn't have worried. We were welcomed like visiting celebrities. The first child who saw us called out, *"Blufono! Blufono!"* ("White man! White man!"). Then, small children came streaming out of doors everywhere, running toward us like the dearest family member returning from a long absence. One brave 3-year-old boy grabbed me by the legs for a hug, and then dozens of others mobbed on, so many that I couldn't move forward for several minutes until I shook the hand of each child and exchanged local greetings.

When I set foot in the school on the first day, the headmaster took me to each of the classrooms for grades one through six. The students jumped up and down and looked to their teacher for the signal to sing the welcoming song they had prepared. As I toured each class, I was serenaded with songs and dances.

One classroom sang "Rise and Shine," a song I knew well from camp. The kids knew the chorus, but not the hand motions or the verses to this well-known American song about Noah and the Flood. Days later

I would teach them the rest of the song and sing it with them until my voice cracked from tears, overwhelmed by their ecstatic and joyful chorus in response to my verses, as we crossed the barriers of distance, race, poverty, language and life experience to unite in a song which cries out, at the top of your lungs, "Rise and shine and give God your glory!"

It's hard to explain how I learned to teach students to read who had, literally, no books at all. Grateful for school buildings (their older siblings learned under trees), the children take turns "sweeping" the schoolroom with bundles of sticks. The map I brought from Accra was the first they had ever seen. I was determined that I would not leave Ghana until each child could pick Ghana out on the map of Africa. The children would gather early before school, excitedly mobbing the map and swapping comments about it in their native tongue. Although I had bought the map for myself, there was no doubt that it had found its permanent home on their otherwise blank schoolroom wall.

Most of the reading and writing occurred off an ancient chalkboard at the front of the room. Without electricity, the teachers could not make copies of lessons or tests, so everything gets written on the board. Chalk was treated as a sacred substance, and the children quickly rescued for future use the tiniest piece of chalk as it broke off from the piece I was using and fell to the floor.

The children worked together to make sure they

all learned as much as possible. One small boy was writing dictation on the board. ("When I grow up, I want to be a doctor" was the hopeful sentence I gave him.) His slightly uphill scrawl eventually made the sentence too high for him to complete. Teetering on tiptoes, he tried to finish the sentence stretching up high. A bigger boy raced to the front of the class and lifted the struggling smaller boy on his shoulders so he could finish the sentence.

Nothing was ever wasted in our little town. At the end of each day, the trash can in my hotel room was filled with wrappers from food, water bottles, used paper products, old receipts, a sock with a hole, etc. However, I noticed that the trash cans in the classrooms never had anything in them — in fact, the only time I ever saw a trash can get used at the school was when one of the children used it as a "basket" during some creative play. In a classroom where the students have one 20-page tablet to last the entire year, there isn't any paper being thrown away. In Ghana, frugality is not a "movement"; it's a necessary life skill.

One day I opened up a disposable camera package in my classroom, which came in an anti-X-ray metal foil packet and was wrapped in a cardboard protective lining. Eager to start taking photos, I ripped open the foil packet and set the cardboard aside. At the end of the school day, the teacher followed me out of the classroom with several students to return the torn foil packet and cardboard lining. When I said I did not want it, the teacher pocketed the foil wrap and gave the cardboard to one lucky student, who called out to his friends about the unexpected gift.

The children never tired of asking questions about how we live in America. "Do you have a telephone? A car?" they asked, in the same tone we might ask someone if he owns a jet or a yacht. My affirmative responses resulted in many, many car drawings being given to me as gifts. I became known as the lady who lived alone and owned her own car, a layer of wealth and extravagance in a town where the only vehicles owned by families were shares in fishing boats.

When we packed to leave, all the participants in my group decided that we would leave everything we could do without in our rooms. We looked at our possessions in a different light now. The mosquito netting which might be saved in a garage pile of camping gear for years at home could save the life of a child here every night. The extra plastic bags could keep food fresher longer, or patch a leaky wall or roof. I devoted a few minutes to tearing the extra unused pages out of my travel journal — some child may be able to practice writing on them. Of course, all medical supplies, down to the last wet wipe and aspirin tablet, were left on the desk, and my travel sheet and pillowcase, and most of my clothes.

Back at home, with more rooms than inhabitants, I now know that God has provided all of my needs, and then some; for all the things I perceived that I lack, I see now I truly have more than enough. First, there are the books — cardboard books for babies, children's books, my own college reading, classics of literature, books written by friends and colleagues, Jewish books, and perhaps most ironically, an entire shelf of books on how to live simply. Two bathrooms, with potable water to brush my teeth and splash on my face. Not having to sterilize my hands after washing my hair in the shower. Hot water, flowing out of the spout! Lights that switch on and off at whim. Stacks of free pads of paper received as promotions from local businesses. Trash cans in every room for the disposal of paper used on one side...plastic bags used once...half-eaten food.

My hot morning shower is like winning the lottery every day. I feel clean again, and leave the house wearing only my skin and clothing designed for modesty, not lifesaving. I hop in my private car and head off to a grocery store, where I am confronted by aisles of cereal, produce and choices, choices, choices, all fresh, easily affordable and safe to eat. At an ATM, I withdraw cash equal to an employed Ghanaian's salary for two months — pocket money for impulse buying.

And yet, I cannot help thinking that I might have stayed longer in our little town. While our days were fraught with challenges, they were purposeful, loving, gracious and without rancor. The children were well mannered, appreciative and always ready to jump up and sing and dance — ready with joy simply when the moment arrived.

In letters they wrote on my last day, they expressed in their rudimentary English a lifetime's worth of feelings: "I am not happy that you are going." "Your songs and teaching are very beautiful." "We love you because you love us." "Thank you for showing us your kindness."

In the months since I visited this tiny coastal town, I have continued to correspond with some of my fifth-grade students there. They unceasingly amaze me with their generosity of spirit and optimism about the future, despite their crushing poverty.

Young Joseph stood out when, in his first letter, he included a single bead as a gift. Beads are a prized local craft, and I let him know in my response that his present touched me deeply. In addition, Joseph was the only student in my school who did not wear a uniform, and although I had never inquired about it, I suspected he just couldn't afford it. So the gift of a painted bead was especially precious to me.

Months later, he wrote me a very different kind of letter. After a lengthy "grace period," the school was now insisting on a uniform, and had suspended him until he could procure one. Sadly, he reported that the required uniform would cost 40,000 cedis — a prohibitively expensive amount for his family, equal to about five U.S. dollars.

Without a uniform, Joseph would be unable to continue his studies beyond the fifth grade — at least not now. I felt the crushing weight of his loss — at best, a delay of months or years before he could return to school; at worst, a life of illiteracy in a country where only the best educated have a chance to break out of the cycle of poverty. Of course, with my next letter, I sent him the five dollars.

I also included one extra dollar which, I explained, was for Joseph to buy another airmail letter and let me know that he had obtained the uniform and was back in school. I knew the extra dollar was more than he needed to write to me, leaving him about 60 cents extra to spend as he wished.

A few weeks later, I was stunned to receive a letter from Joseph in a small package. "I thank you very much for what you have done for me," he wrote, "and I do not even know how to thank you. If it were not for you, I would not have my school uniform. May God bless you and your family and also give you a long life."

I have grown accustomed to the flowery words of gratitude which accompany every letter from my students — appreciation seems to be a national trait. But I was unprepared for what else the package contained. With the extra 60 cents, Joseph had purchased more beads, and made a necklace, a bracelet and matching earrings for me, to show his appreciation.

I would have been happy if he had bought himself a small treat, or surprised his family with some fresh fruit or a few eggs. I probably would have preferred if he had bought some pencils or other small school supplies, or a gift for his mother who had recently broken her leg. I had wondered how he would use the extra money, but it had never occurred to me that he would use it to thank me.

I'm not much of a jewelry person, and beads are not really my style, but these have become the accessory I reach for first and most often. I feel more fully human when I wear them, connected to a soul truly free of materialism. For a child who quite simply has nothing — his family could not scrape together five dollars to keep him in school — he has something most people lack. He knows that having a little more money, a few more things, would not change the core of whether he was happy or not — and that a sincere expression of gratitude most certainly would.

RABBI NECHEMIA COOPERSMITH

RAISING YEHUDA

lthough the Almighty gives us all just what we need, sometimes it takes a good deal of soul searching to recognize His blessings. Six weeks after my wife gave birth to our son, who has Down syndrome, I am beginning to appreciate that we are the recipients of a precious gift.

This realization did not come right away. In fact, the first time I stood staring at our newborn son, as he lay in the neonatal unit surrounded by machines, awaiting surgery to repair an intestinal blockage, the overwhelming feeling I had was disbelief.

This was not who we were hoping would be our

Rabbi Nechemia Coopersmith lives in Jerusalem with his wife and children. He is the chief editor of Aish.com and the author of Shmooze: A Guide to Thought-Provoking Discussion on Essential Jewish Issues — a must-have little book for anyone who loves a good question.

fourth child; this was not the son who would grow up to be a Torah scholar. Instead, I suddenly became the father of a retarded boy who was going to be dependent on me for the rest of my life. It felt like God must have made some kind of mistake. I was sick to my stomach and in a state of daze and confusion.

I woke up the next morning hoping everything was just some kind of terrible dream. *This can't really be happening...*

But it was.

"I may be mistaken, but I believe your son has Down's," Dr. Gur explained to me shortly after the birth of the baby. I sat across from the doctor, looking right at him as he spoke to me, but I might as well have been a thousand miles away. "He has some of the classic signs — slanted eyes and duodenal atresia, an intestinal malformation that 30 percent of the time means Down's. But we can't be sure until we get the results back from the chromosome test, which will take at least a week."

"But all of our children were born with Oriental eyes...it's a strong familial trait," I countered. "And he *is* missing some of the telltale signs."

"I hope I'm wrong. We'll have to wait for the test results to know for certain."

Late that night, I spoke to my rabbi, Rabbi Noah Weinberg, for much-needed counsel. "Think about how you and Dina would change if you were to have a child with Down's," he advised me. "What is the growth the Almighty would want from you? You have a week before you get the results; make those changes now."

We clung to the slight chance that the baby was in fact just fine. Although Jews do not rely on outright miracles, we can pray for "hidden miracles" — events that do not require a complete turning over of the laws of nature.

During those seven days, I experienced an intensity in prayer that I never had before. For the first time I truly understood what the Psalmist describes when he says, "I am my prayer to You" (Psalms 69:14). Genuine prayer occurs when one's entire being, heart and soul, cries out to God with such an aching, ever-present need, that the person himself becomes an expression of prayer. It didn't matter where I was or what I was doing, there was nothing else on my mind but crying out to God.

And it was a total solitary experience; no one knew what my wife and I were going through. In order to keep the hoped-for miracle hidden from view, we decided to keep the possibility of Down's to ourselves until we got the final results. Our friends attributed all of our stress to the baby's surgery and recovery in the hospital, which to us was just a minor detail in the big scheme of things.

On the second morning, I awoke, startled by a dream. I dreamt that I was being chased by a menacing figure. I was running as fast as I could through winding mountainous paths, desperately trying to get away, but the threatening presence was always one or two steps right behind, about to pounce. Since I couldn't outrun it, I realized that the only way to save myself was to turn around and confront it, head on.

I stopped suddenly, turned on my heels and came face-to-face with the ominous creature. "I'm not going to hurt you," he said as he reached out his hand. "I'm here to teach you..."

I'm not the type who places much significance in dreams, but this dream's message hit me loud and clear: "Don't run away from the baby; embrace him. The Almighty has sent him for your good."

That morning, as my shock began to fade, my attitudes began to undergo further changes. I was standing over our baby, who had just been transferred to another hospital for his surgery. It was the first time I was able to look at him without all the machinery surrounding him. He was sleeping peacefully, and as I stroked his head I was overcome with a wave of sympathy for my sweet and utterly defenseless son. Suddenly I was stung by the realization of how self-absorbed I'd been. What do my disappointment and unmet expectations matter, I realized. This baby desperately needs me. Get with the program!

When I changed my focus away from me and toward giving to my baby son, I forgot all about the possibility of Down's. By doing whatever I could to help him, I began to feel buoyed by the natural love a parent has for his child.

We spent that week in the hospital while our son

recuperated. ("Your son is a real fighter," the surgeon told me. "We've never seen a baby recover so quickly from this type of surgery.") All that time, sitting next to the crib of my sleeping infant, gave me opportunity to reconsider a lot of things: my views on parenting, what kind of meaningful life a person can lead if he has cognitive limitations, and the changes I would need to make in order to properly raise a child with Down's.

I realized that a primary aspect of my parenting is the honor I receive from my children's success and accomplishments. I was suffering from a religious version of "my-son-the-doctor" syndrome. Instead of the pride and respect I would accrue from being the father of children who went on to become successful, wealthy professionals, I was banking on their success in being the best in Torah learning and Jewish leadership. In both cases, an underlying drive is how children will go on to fulfill the dreams of the parents and boost their status. My respect for my children was linked, to some extent, to their accomplishments.

Every parent knows this attitude is wrong, but it's extremely difficult to uproot. It's not easy to love our children unconditionally, to focus solely on helping them bring their unique potentials to fruition. What happens when their potential is so much less or so very different than we had hoped?

Our child is not here to fulfill our needs and expectations. The Almighty gave him to us as an entrustment, charging me and my wife with the holy task of helping him achieve his special mission in life. That is our job as parents, whether the child is born a genius or impaired with Down's.

But what kind of purpose in life can our son have if he is mentally impaired? This question forced me to confront another fallacious value that my wife and I shared (along with most of Western society). We put far too much value on intelligence. We tend to place greater importance on being smart than being good. My son may not excel in learning and academics, but he can excel in becoming a *tzaddik*, a righteous Jew who sincerely cares about others and strives to fulfill the Torah's commandments to the best of his ability. And that, after all, is the true measure of a person.

My agitation about my son's possible mental limitations revealed far more about my limitations than his.

Don't get me wrong. We still expect a lot from our son. We decided right from the start that the best approach to dealing with any inborn disabilities is to expect the most until proven otherwise. But our *nachas* isn't going to come from our son doing better than others; it will come from his striving to attain personal milestones as he works hard to fulfill his unique potential.

The day before our son was discharged from the hospital, the geneticist confirmed the diagnosis of Down syndrome. I was taken aback by the results. After a week of incredibly intensive praying that our son would not have the chromosome disorder, and trying to work on making the changes I thought the Almighty wanted from me, I was really expecting that everything would be just fine.

I had to make a major mental readjustment. Looking at the big picture, I realized that God had given my wife and me a daunting task, and if we were to rise to the challenge of raising our special son, we — and our extended families — would be better for it. Perhaps for the first time that week, I not only intellectually thought that God knew what was truly best for us, but I finally felt it in my bones. Everything, in fact, would be just fine.

Rabbi Moshe Shapiro, a leading Torah scholar in Jerusalem, wrote the following letter to a student who became the father of a son with Down's:

> *Since the birth of your son, Nota Shlomo, I have believed that if, with God's help, you will succeed in the challenge which was given to you, then you will have been presented with an incomparable gift.*
>
> *This child has within him the capability to accomplish that which nothing else in the world can do — to actualize wondrous and powerful energy latent in the recesses of your heart.*

The Almighty also knows what is best for our son. The fact that he was born with limited cognitive abilities indicates that he possesses a lofty soul that is in need of less rectification in this world.

Rabbi Shapiro wrote in the same letter:

> *Each soul is sent to this world with the purpose of*

rectifying something specific to it. Most people are sent to improve themselves primarily, and also to affect their surroundings according to their abilities. There are some souls, however, which are sent as people incapable of adequately rectifying themselves. In defining their existence, then, we must understand that these are especially exalted souls which in and of themselves need no correction. Their entire purpose in being sent to this world is to correct and better their surroundings.

A soul of this grand stature has been sent into your home. Accept it with much love, and assist it to perform the function for which it was sent.

May God help you to carry out your role — to enable this soul to suitably fulfill its role.

We named our son Yehuda Meir, which can be translated literally as "a shining source of gratitude."

One of the clear lessons his life has already taught us is to appreciate every tiny step that we usually take for granted. When Yehuda Meir, at six weeks, turned his head and rolled over (the physical therapists didn't believe us at first!), it became a spontaneous household celebration. Every small milestone in his life — from smiling to sitting up to walking and talking — will be viewed as a massive accomplishment and a gift from the Almighty. We can't take *anything* for granted, including our son's general good health (50 percent of children with Down syndrome have congenital heart defects). And we're trying to direct this heightened appreciation to our other children as well.

The name "Yehuda" also contains the Hebrew word *hod*, which means majestic beauty and splendor. *Hod* is a special form of beauty that occurs when the internal spiritual value far exceeds the external package, and breaks through, bursting at the seams and overwhelming the physical.

For example, when Moses came down from Mount Sinai, rays of light — in Hebrew *karnei hod* — exuded from his face and no one could look at his awe-inspiring presence. This burst of light represented Moses' inner spiritual dimension that could not be contained by his physical exterior. His inner spirituality broke through and surpassed his physical limitations, revealing a spiritual essence far greater than his small, earthly self could contain.

Each and every one of us is given a set of certain strengths and limitations that create our special mission in life. Our work in this world is to strive to reach beyond our limitations and make our life a glowing source of *hod*, of majestic beauty — which is the meaning of the name "Yehuda Meir."

This applies equally to our little Yehuda Meir, whose limitations are more pronounced. While he may not attain quantitatively an equal share of Torah and leadership skills as some great rabbis, he can strive to attain an equal share *qualitatively* — not despite his inherent limitations, but by specifically using them as a springboard to let his special inner beauty burst forth. Yehuda Meir, no less than any Jew, can become a radiant source of Godliness in the world.

My wife and I still catch ourselves tripping over the misplaced value of intelligence over goodness, thinking to ourselves how our son will be one of the smartest, most accomplished children with Down syndrome. We realize we have a lot of growth and challenge — and most of all, joy! — ahead. We are taking great pleasure (along with our other kids) in getting to know our adorable son, and pray that the Almighty will give us the clarity, patience and wisdom to carry out our noble task in raising this precious Jewish soul.

SARAH ZELDMAN

THE SELFISH SHABBAT

I wish I could say that I began to observe Shabbat because I'm such a spiritual person and yearned to connect with God. But that would be a lie. I hardly believed in God's existence when I started to observe Shabbat.

I also wish I could say that I began to observe Shabbat after experiencing really cool things like meditating with the Buddhists and dancing with the Sufis. But that too would be a lie. I didn't search other religions on a quest for spiritual truth before I explored Judaism.

Sarah Zeldman is a life and business coach, motivating busy women to restore balance, order, energy and fun to their hectic lives — at SolutionsForBusyMoms.com.

I began to observe Shabbat for only one reason: I was selfish.

I looked around me and saw friends and family who never knew when to stop working. I saw friends who were depressed and wondering, "Is this what life is all about?" But they suppressed the question in various ways because they did not know where to look for answers.

I saw families come apart at the seams, partly due to a commitment to the "pursuit of happiness" (read: financial wealth) at the expense of a commitment to family life and spiritual growth. I saw a society that more and more tragically reflected the consequence of these decisions.

So I began to observe Shabbat, because I wanted a better life.

But first a little background. Until the age of 12, I received a typical Jewish day school education. My family sometimes had Friday night dinners, kept kosher at home and celebrated major holidays. I loved being Jewish, but Judaism was not really part of my daily life.

After my Bat Mitzvah, most of our observances faded into the background, until I arrived at college. There I was involved with Hillel (where else do you meet the nice Jewish boys?), but I really wasn't interested in Judaism per se. I figured I had been there, done that, and it wasn't very interesting or inspiring. I thought that I knew pretty much all there was to learn. And as is often the case with many day school graduates, my childhood knowledge of Judaism did not satisfy the needs of my adult mind.

Then I picked up a book called *Jewish Literacy* by Rabbi Joseph Telushkin. Everything changed. From that book, I learned that there was a lot I didn't know about Judaism, that there was literally a whole treasure chest of wisdom just waiting for me.

So I asked and asked and asked. I spoke to people from all streams of Judaism: Reconstructionist, Reform, Conservative — even those crazy Orthodox people that my dad did business with. I went on Jewish learning programs and read and read and read some more. Eventually I couldn't refuse the invitations of our observant friends anymore, so I joined them for Shabbat.

I remember the car ride over there. I went through a checklist of things like: "Now, these people are observant, so wear a skirt, watch your language, don't turn lights on and off, and just try to make it through this boring weekend with a smile."

But what I found was anything but boring. What I saw actually moved me to tears. I saw a family, not just a bunch of people biologically related to each other, but a family of people *relating* to each other. I saw a family truly united by the knowledge that for the next 24 hours, they had nowhere to go and were thus totally committed to interacting with each other — no business to conduct, no shopping to do, no phone calls to return.

Looking into the eyes of those children, I saw an

innocence and security that I had not seen in the secular world. And I saw a satisfaction and relaxation in the parents which is so rare today. With everyone and everything dressed in their Shabbat best, and an atmosphere of total freedom in the air (that is, freedom from the mundane), I then understood why it is said, "More than the Jews have kept the Shabbat, Shabbat has kept the Jews."

However, admiring Shabbat and keeping all the laws that make the atmosphere so special are two different things. Eventually I decided that I wanted Shabbat in my life, and I wanted it for my future family. So sometime in my junior year of college, I said to an observant friend, "Okay, Sussie. I have good news and bad news: The good news is that I want to start keeping Shabbat. The bad news is that I'm not doing it until after I graduate from college!"

Of all the mitzvot, I wanted Shabbat and only Shabbat — like an item from a menu. Just Shabbat.

That's when my journey really began. Instead of just reading about Judaism, I started living it, step by step. The first Shabbat after I graduated from college, I didn't go anywhere. Not to the mall, to the movies or out with my friends. I stayed at home, cooked, built bookshelves and watched TV — lots of things that an observant Jew wouldn't do on Shabbat! But I didn't go out.

After a few weeks of this, a friend said to me, "Sarah, that's good, but Shabbat isn't just about not doing things. It's also about *yes* doing things. Why don't you go to shul next week?"

The next Shabbat, I walked to shul, where I was completely lost in a sea of Hebrew. I just couldn't wait for them to get to some prayers I knew from my childhood, especially *Aleinu*. Not because I liked that prayer so much, but because *Aleinu* would signal that services were almost over!

I survived the service, but afterward something unexpected happened. Many families, before they even knew my name, invited me for Shabbat lunch, dinner, Passover and Chanukah next year if I was free. This was a new experience for me. I wondered, "Who are these people and how could they invite me, a stranger, into their home?"

My first reaction was, "Um...can I see some ID, please?" Later I learned that they were doing something very normal, the mitzvah of *hachnasat orchim* — welcoming guests. This mitzvah made my process of observing Shabbat so much easier. I would go home with these families for lunch and enjoy my time there. Then I would go home and turn on all the lights — just to show that I could!

Over the course of a year, I eventually stopped turning on the lights, stopped using the phone, etc. I had been true to my vow in college to become Shabbat observant. That was where it was supposed to end. But like a steady drip of water can eventually carve into a large boulder, so too Torah can enter the heart of someone as stubborn as me.

After being with Torah observant families every

Shabbat for a year, I wanted more. If this one mitzvah could enhance my personal and family life so much, maybe other mitzvot could, too. Of course, being as I was selfish and my observance had nothing to do with God, I wasn't going to do any mitzvah that was too difficult or didn't promise to enhance my life.

But I found that I couldn't keep God out of the picture for long. I was regularly around families with their beautiful faith and connection to God, and I knew that if I just continued doing the mitzvot for me alone, I couldn't sustain all the positive changes I had made in my life. And I certainly wouldn't be able to pass them on to the next generation.

That's when I left for Israel to study at yeshiva. I went on a quest to get my questions answered and break down the walls of doubt and fear standing in the way of my connection with God. It was a long road between who I was when I got on that plane and the woman I am now, who speaks to God daily to ask Him for strength and guidance.

These days, I often meet 20-somethings and see in them myself. I want to tell them gently: If you think that you know all there is to know about Judaism, think again. Not even the greatest rabbi knows everything there is to know about Torah. Pick up a book. Or better yet, take a class. Don't rely on your childhood knowledge of Judaism. Make a commitment to study Judaism as an adult. You'll be surprised, both by what you didn't know, and by what you thought you knew.

And for those who, like me, find the mitzvot so beautiful but are overwhelmed by their number and complexity, start with just one mitzvah. Torah life is not an all-or-nothing proposition. Start wherever you want to. Memorize one blessing and use it. Stop doing housework on Shabbat. Make a commitment to learn more about Torah.

Most importantly, keep on thinking, learning and asking questions. If you take one step closer toward God, then His strength and love, reflected through the mitzvot, will take you the rest of the way.

MIRIAM KATZ

THE SCAM

You know those e-mail scams that use some flimsy excuse to ask for your credit card number? Did you ever wonder who would be stupid enough to actually provide the requested information? Well, I have a confession to make...

Last week, I received an e-mail message asking that I update my Internet account information in order to prevent my e-mail address from being deactivated. Ever the dutiful consumer, I clicked on the attached link and filled out the form completely: name, address, date of birth, PIN, credit card number. I pressed SEND and felt pleased that I had dealt with the issue so promptly.

It was only several moments later that the first

Miriam Katz is a freelance writer, editor and teacher. She lives with her husband in Jerusalem.

doubt crossed my mind. Had that e-mail message *really* come from my Internet provider? Why did they need so much information, anyway? A closer examination of the sender's address confirmed my suspicions.

The foolish consumers who fall for these things are, apparently, people like me. Dismayed, I went straight to the phone and cancelled my credit card.

I've always been naive. As a child, when my babysitter claimed that the word "gullible" wasn't in the dictionary, I went to the bookshelf and triumphantly proved her wrong before I got the joke. This time, however, my cluelessness could have had far more drastic consequences. How could I have failed to spot the warning signs, especially when these scams are so prevalent? What planet do I live on?

It's difficult for me to be distrustful of others — and the neighborhood that I recently moved into doesn't help, either. My community is plagued by such rampant, uncontrolled kindness that suspicion is hard to come by.

My neighbors cook for women who have just given birth and happily allow strangers to stay in their apartments when they go away for Shabbat. Many people run free loan societies out of their homes, where chairs, pacifiers, medical equipment and moving boxes are lent out to people in need. A nearby family leaves the front door of their ground-floor apartment unlocked — even when no one is home — because they expect a stream of people to come by at all hours: returning pots and pans, borrowing books and picking up keys.

In this neighborhood it doesn't take a disaster to get us to drop our defenses and join together. It is actually *expected* that people will offer support on a daily basis and help each other out.

The status quo in today's world is decidedly different. More often than not, suspicion is the norm, and we term "naive" those people who display less than the accepted level of distrust. We listen skeptically to sales people; we pore over the fine print before signing on the dotted line; and we teach our children not to accept candy from strangers. We assume that others are primarily concerned with their own self-interests — and unfortunately, our suspicions are often justified.

In college, my roommate was once intrigued by an advertisement that promised to pay good money for work done at home. The exact nature of this work was unclear, and when my friend called for more information, she was told to send a $20 fee in order to receive introductory materials. This sounded fishy to me, and I told her so; nevertheless, she mailed off her check.

The letter she received in return stunned us both. It said, unabashedly, "This was a scam. But don't feel bad. Here are instructions for how you can create your own scam and cheat other people."

I recognize the need to take precautions and to cultivate a certain degree of skepticism. But there is a cost to spending our lives second-guessing the motives of everyone we encounter. It's all too easy to slip from an attitude of basic distrust into a pervasive outlook of cynicism and bitterness. When we expect the worst from any situation, we are surprised by good. We think: How remarkable — that child got up so that an elderly lady could sit down! How shocking — he drove miles out of his way to direct me to my destination! Even small acts of kindness have become so unexpected that they startle us.

Yet this is entirely backwards. Treating each other with respect and generosity ought to be the norm, not the exception. We should be shocked by scams, not by kindness.

After sending off my credit card information to those Internet crooks, instead of getting angry at myself for being so trusting, I had a moment of honest confusion. Why would someone want to swindle another person? How could a human being put so much effort into stealing someone else's money? My bewilderment at the deception lasted much longer than the frustration over my own foolishness. For the first time, I felt a clear sense of What Should Be — not as indignation or outrage, but as simple fact. I can't remember ever feeling so innocent.

It took my Internet naiveté to help me recognize what I value about living among Jews. I remember how a friend of mine, perplexed at my move toward greater Jewish observance, questioned me frankly before I left for Israel. "I don't understand," she said, "why do you want to go live around people who are exactly like you?"

I did not choose to live in this neighborhood because of the superficial similarities between myself and my neighbors. The people in my community are *not* all like me — but they are in many ways exactly the way I'd *like* to be. My neighbors tend to be trusting and trustworthy. They manifest the values that I hold dear. Living here, I am gradually starting to expect the best from others, and that is reawakening my moral sensitivity. What more could I ask for?

I do not yet lend out medical equipment or baby supplies from my home, and when I run errands, I still lock the door. But in a strange way, I am proud that I fell for that Internet scam. Of course, I'll be more cautious next time; I've learned my lesson. But I'm glad that my instinctive response is to trust the sincere intentions of others, even when it makes me look foolish. In a culture where skepticism is the norm, I'd much rather be bewildered by corruption than compassion.

ARNOLD ROTH

AGE FIFTEEN

M ost Jewish teenagers growing up in Australia during the 1960s were, like me, children of concentration camp survivors. Our parents owned small businesses or were employed. There was hardly a professional among them. At birth, we lacked even a single grandparent in most cases, and almost all of us were named after family members who perished at the hands of the Nazis.

It was clear that we were "everything" to our parents, and no one needed to tell us why. Top of their priority list was ensuring that we gained the best possible education. Little wonder that several of the

Arnold Roth is an attorney living in Jerusalem. He also heads the Malki Foundation (www. kerenmalki.org), in memory of his daughter, which helps families provide severely disabled children with quality home care.

largest and most successful Jewish schools in the world were started in Melbourne in the years right after World War II. And the community's interest in things Israeli was unlimited — the occasional Israeli film and Israeli visitor to Australia's distant shores were memorable events.

The Six Day War happened when I was 15. The weeks of rising tension leading up to it left an indelible mark on me: the grainy television images of Egyptian and Syrian troops on the march; Nasser's strident speeches and unilateral blockade of the sea lanes to Eilat; the massing of Egyptian forces on Israel's Sinai border and of the Syrians on the Golan frontier; U Thant's disgraceful capitulation in removing UN peace-keeping forces from Sinai precisely when they were most needed. And the blood-curdling threats of one after another of the Arab dictators and monarchs: "The existence of Israel is an error which must be rectified... This is our opportunity to erase the ignominy which has been with us since 1948... Our goal is clear — to wipe Israel off the map."

Fifteen marked a turning point in my life. A few months after Israel's stunning defeat of the forces bent (once again) on the liquidation of the Jews, I enrolled for the first time in a Jewish day school. My ideas about being a Jew in the world, about history and how it affects our lives, about the Holocaust and the chain of Jewish life, began taking grown-up shape.

My mother grew up near Lodz in a town located

close enough to the Polish-German frontier to have been overrun by Nazi forces on the first day of the war. Among the men rounded up by the invaders on that September day was her father, the grandfather whose name I was given. As a father myself, I have to breathe deeply in calling to mind the image of my mother throwing herself at the feet of a German soldier, begging, screaming for her father's life to be spared.

On the day the Nazis marched into Poland and began the process of destroying a world, trampling a unique culture into the mud, murdering Jews by the millions, my mother had just turned 15.

My awareness of my parents' lives begins, in a certain sense, with the end of the war: their four or five years as displaced persons in post-war Germany, their long journey to Australia as a young couple with no English, no marketable skills and no roots beyond their few personal ties and their very Jewish sense of community.

An unexpected photograph changed this for me a few years ago.

I have a cousin, a kibbutznik, the daughter of my father's oldest brother. She was brought to Tel Aviv in the 1930s as a baby by her parents who fled pre-war Galicia, and has lived her life in Israel. Returning as a tourist to her roots, she traveled to Krakow in 2000, and via a chain of circumstances ended up in possession of four photocopied pages which she shared with me. These were Nazi documents — census forms which the Germans required the Jews in the Krakow ghetto to complete prior to dispatching them to the death camps.

The first page had been completed in the distinctive handwriting of my father, of blessed memory. A small snapshot attached to the form showed him as I had never seen before: virile, handsome, young. Two other pages were the census forms of two of my father's sisters. Their names were known to me from a family tree I had put together years earlier with my father's help, but until that moment they were nothing more than names. Now I gazed at the portraits of two vibrant young women.

My oldest daughter, Malki, had just completed a family-roots project at school, and I knew she would be interested. A glance at the pages and she said exactly what I had been thinking: Malki bore a striking resemblance to my father's beautiful sister Feige.

Unlike my parents, Feige did not survive the Nazi murder machine. Whatever promise her life contained, whatever talents she was developing, whatever gifts she was planning to give the world — all these were overturned by a massive act of violent, barbaric hatred.

Some months after we gazed on those extraordinary pictures for the first time, Malki sat down and quietly (without telling us) composed the words and music of an infectiously upbeat song: "You live, breathe and move. That's a great start!... You'd better start dancing now!"

Living in the land promised to the Jewish people was a source of deep contentment to this grand-daughter of Holocaust survivors. The discovery of Feige's picture enabled Malki, I think, to gain a strengthened sense of her personal role as a link in an ancient chain.

Arafat's intifada war against Israel's civilian population broke out around the time we received those precious pages. From the diary she kept, it's evident that the near-daily toll of injuries and deaths weighed heavily on Malki's mind. She writes of having to leave her classroom to weep in privacy upon learning of another terror attack... and another and another. We, her parents and siblings, were unaware of the depth of her empathy for the victims of the war raging in her precious land. The turmoil and pain, to Malki, were deeply personal. Though born in Australia, she had lived in Jerusalem since age two. She felt deeply connected to Jewish history.

In August 2001, my daughter and her friend Michal interrupted the activities of a busy summer vacation day to grab lunch in a crowded Jerusalem restaurant, Sbarro.

If she had noticed the man with a guitar case on his back striding through the unguarded door and positioning himself next to the counter where she was engrossed in tapping out a text message on her cell phone, would Malki have recognized the hatred, the barbaric ecstasy, on his face before he exploded?

Malki and Michal were buried the next day. The

closest of friends since early childhood, they lie side by side, forever, on a hill near the entrance to Jerusalem.

Malki was 15.

Her diary is full of questions: How can such terrible things happen to our people? Why is our love for the Land of Israel not better understood by outsiders? What kind of Divine plan calls for teenagers to be injured and killed by people for whom we hold no hatred at all? How can such intense hatred even exist?

The unbearable question marks left behind by my daughter scream at me every day.

Jewish life, viewed from a distance, is an astonishing saga of tragedy, achievement, grandeur, destruction and greatness, played out over millennia. There is a risk we lose this perspective when we are the individuals living it.

At Purim, we feast, we drink, we ceremoniously deliver gifts, we celebrate with those we love and like. But the narrative at the heart of this festival is of a close brush with tragedy: the Jewish victory over a genocidal conspiracy by murderous Jew-haters.

Here in Jerusalem, a day later than almost everywhere else in the world, Purim is marked on the 15th day of Adar. Jewish calendar dates are written using a simple alphanumeric code: *alef* is one, *bet* is two and so on. But longstanding tradition is to avoid the straightforward way of writing the number 15. You would expect it to be *yud-heh* (lit., ten-five); however these

77

two letters happen to form the first half of God's name and are accorded special treatment and respect.

Accordingly, 15 is written as *tet-vav*: nine-six. God's name, as it were, is hidden within the number 15.

Purim is odd in another way: the name of God is completely absent from *Megillat Esther*. Does this mean the victory of the Jews over their oppressor happened without His involvement? Jewish tradition answers with a firm "no." God's role was crucial, but our ability to make sense of how and why He acts is limited, inadequate.

Those of us raised in the shadow of the Holocaust, and who have experienced the tragedy of a child's death by hatred, struggle to understand the nature of the Divine role in our lives as individuals and as a people. There are times, according to Jewish wisdom, when you need to know that God's hand is at work even when the evidence is difficult to see, even when there are more questions than answers.

REBECCA APPELSON

STUCK BEING SINGLE

When I was a little girl at summer camp, I'd send my mother the first letter on July 10 reminding her that my birthday was three month's hence.

August 10, September 10... all were days leading up to that magical one: October 10, the anniversary of my entry into the world.

On the morning of my birthday, I would wake to a house festooned with banners and balloons, all proclaiming, "Rebecca is eight!" "Happy Birthday, Beck!" "We love the birthday girl!" Depending on whatever color I loved that year, they'd be green or pink or blue or magenta, and my mother would be waiting with some sort of particularly elaborate

---

Rebecca Appelson is a pseudonym of a writer who lives in Jerusalem.

breakfast and the whole day would be spent celebrating...me.

On November 10, I'd remind her that she had only 11 months left to plan for the next one.

How and how those were the days.

These days, on August 10, my eyes skit away from the calendar. By September 10, I sigh deeply and begin the month-long process of bracing myself. In the week leading up to October 10, I try to steel myself for it, and — new tactic — even try to convince myself that I am happy about the day.

It's not that I am another year older... it's not that my life is passing me by without moving forward (my nieces and nephews are another year older, stunningly old — kids now, no longer babies). I tell myself that lives aren't measured only by being married and having children. My life is rich, full of friends and family, a great job, and I even have the privilege of living in Israel — fulfilling a life-long dream. I can look back at the last five years and claim real achievements — emotional growth, solidified relationships with family, goals met.

But, somehow, when October 10 rolls around, all I see is the fact that I am no longer the little girl thrilling to magenta balloons...that I don't have anyone to make special breakfasts for, the way my mom made them for me.

It's a burden the rest of the year. I feel it, and when the yearning occasionally overpowers me — for an hour sometimes, and sometimes for a day, sometimes longer — I am sickened with myself. There is so much good in my life, and yet all I see is the lack. There is so much good in my life, and yet, sometimes, every moment aches.

Believe it or not, I have a naturally happy disposition. And, sometimes, when I am taken over with longing for a life other than the one I have — work, home, work, home, date, doesn't work out, work, home — I wonder just what it is that women who don't have the incredible blessing of a sunny outlook go through. What do their days look like to them? How do they manage to get themselves out of bed — to another day that just seems to remind you with every moment that, for whatever reason, you can't have what you think you were created for? Why did God give me such a loving nature if I wasn't meant to have people to give to, and people to spoil — the best way to be challenged and grow?

And, yes, monotony, and struggles, and disappointments. Because being married and being a mother doesn't mean that your life suddenly becomes easy and perfect. If anything, it brings with it a set of enormous challenges that I can fathom only because I've watched so many of my friends struggle with them.

My life is my own — marriage and especially motherhood make you utterly beholden to others. A wife must always consider her husband, and a mother must always, in some ways, give her life over to the needs of her children. Their schedules, their requirements, their moods...they dictate the ins and outs of nearly every moment of their mother's day.

There's no more leisurely reading, no more running out at the drop of a hat, no more deciding to go somewhere on a whim. Sleeping through the night becomes a major accomplishment.

And yet, I think, it must all be so utterly worth it when your child opens up his eyes and sees you there in the morning.

So I remind myself of this: of my independence, of the way that I can expand my mind and challenge it while it is still free of concerns over bottle temperatures and peanut allergies. I can still go to a lecture without worrying about tracking down a babysitter. I can make what I want for dinner or not bother going shopping for two weeks. I can sleep late and go away on weekends and dispose of my disposable income however I like.

I even try to convince myself that dating is fun — after all, almost all the men I've ever gone out with are good and kind, if not the man I should marry — and that my life has an excitement and variation my married friends somehow envy. After all, they sometimes tell me this.

And I see how hard marriage can sometimes be, and how one is forced to grow, accommodate and bite one's tongue. It's not all wine and roses.

And still I long for the days when I will roll my eyes because my husband, yet again, didn't change the toilet roll, or is being a pig-headed guy, or has his annoying friends over again.

On those days, will I remember how I cried at night after another date with someone else who wasn't "him," wondering how on earth I am ever going to find the man with whom I'm going to build my life?

Will I remember the frustration of trying again? Will I even recognize him when he does come? Or will I be so beaten down by the weight of all this, of all this longing and impatience and yearning and frustration, that I won't even recognize him when he finally appears?

What I wonder the most is how I can bear all this — all this whining and kvetching and feeling ridiculously sorry for myself — and still be a bearable person? People tell me that I am cheery and sunny and funny, and men I've dated have even paid me the dear compliment that unlike so many other "women my age," I'm "not bitter." The sadness inside me apparently has eaten away only that which is too deep to be seen.

The worst thing is that those who are closest to me know, and must feel, the murk and the whining and the oh-so-not-sunny part.

A friend who just suffered a miscarriage — her second in a half a year — told me that sometimes she feels that if someone touched her, she might crumble away from sadness. My heart went out to her; she is so good, and I don't know any better than she does why God sends such challenges her way.

I admire her courage though... and her steadfast belief that whatever comes to us is somehow necessary for the growth we have to do in life.

There are times when I feel like it's enough. I've grown enough from these challenges. I'm ready to move on to the next set.

And when I do, when I am annoyed with my husband and exhausted from the kids, I just hope that I'll be able to remember what I feel now...and be grateful, so grateful, for what I'll have then.

YISRAEL RUTMAN

THE ROYAL JEW FROM SWAZILAND

The story of every convert to Judaism is a gripping tale of spiritual discovery. In the case of Natan Gamedze, that journey began 40 years ago in Swaziland, where he was born into a royal family.

Gamedze casts an imposing royal figure, but it is his intellectual capacity that makes the biggest impression. Graduated with honors from Oxford, he received a master's in translation from South Africa's Wits University, and served as translator in the Supreme Court of South Africa.

Yisrael Rutman lives in Israel, where he teaches Jewish studies, edits E-geress.org, and writes for various publications.

After many years of study, Gamedze is now a rabbi and teaches Jewish studies in the northern Israeli city of Tzfat where he lives with his wife and son.

Aish.com: Let's begin by verifying facts. Is it true about your being an African prince?

Gamedze: I am indeed. I grew up in Swaziland until the age of 8. It's a small, land-locked kingdom that borders on South Africa and Mozambique — about the size of Israel, with just over a million people.

A: Were you in line for the throne yourself?

G: My grandfather was king. But the British, who had colonized southern Africa, created the states of Swaziland, Bosutoland and Bechuanaland. They drew artificial borders, very often failing to take into consideration the ethnic distribution. So in many places, different ethnic groups were lumped together in the same state. That is what happened to us. And the British chose to recognize a rival royal family as the ruling group.

In order to win our cooperation, they made certain concessions to our family — such as granting ministerial posts — and we have a semi-autonomous region within Swaziland. My father served as minister of education and ambassador to the EEC countries. Today, it's more like a paramount chief than a king, but they do wield power.

A: Which languages do you speak?

G: I speak 13 languages: French, German, Italian, English, Hebrew, Afrikaans, Zulu, and other African languages. Everyone in my family speaks at least two European languages; my mom speaks about seven or eight.

A: It is unusual, to say the least, for someone of your background to find his way to Judaism.

G: I was never interested in religion, per se. I was interested in what was going on in the world. What is our reason for being here? Okay, so you get up in the morning, you eat, go to work, have a shower, watch TV, go to bed, get up and start all over again... Hey, I did that yesterday!

I felt that life was like being on a conveyer belt, and eventually you get off. So what was the point? I couldn't accept that.

A: An existential question.

G: Yes. In other words, I wasn't searching for a way to give my life meaning. Rather, I was trying to find out what was going on, like a detective. I felt there's something going on in this world, something behind the scenes. And I wanted to know what it is.

A: If you weren't looking for religion, how did you find it?

G: I was sitting in a boring Italian literature class one day. I think we were studying D'Annunzio. And as people do when they are bored, they look around, and

I noticed some guy was writing backwards in funny letters. So after class I asked him what he was doing. He said he was doing his Hebrew homework. I thought: *That's really interesting. Imagine if I could write like that!* And then I forgot about it. But later on, I needed a credit to complete my degree. I wanted to take Russian, but I had a scheduling conflict. Then I remembered about Hebrew. It fit my schedule, and so I began studying it.

A: So what was the moment of awakening?

G: The first text we got was the biblical passage of the Binding of Isaac. Coming as I did from a moderately Christian home, I was familiar with the text, but I was surprised at how Hebrew appeared to convey much more than could be conveyed in any other language. I couldn't figure it out.

But what was so compelling was that it was like opening an inner dimension that perhaps many people don't even know exists. It wasn't like an archeologist trying to find out about, say, ancient Incas, an interest which has really nothing to do with him. Here, I felt it was telling me something about myself. I thought it had to do with the language itself. I didn't know at the time it was the religious dimension.

A: And from there?

G: I began to discover the beauty of Judaism. I got interested in Maimonides' *Mishneh Torah*. I would carry it around and read it and tell my Jewish friends about it, who later became observant. It was a bit strange that the very person who was bringing them closer to Judaism wasn't Jewish.

But it was frustrating. I couldn't understand why I had such a thirst and love for Judaism, and not be Jewish. And yet there were Jewish people who couldn't care less, it appeared. Not only that, but when they did decide to get interested, it was easy for them. The opportunity was right there. I asked myself: *Why am I out of the picture?* I couldn't understand why God would play such a trick on me.

At that point, I figured the best thing would be to get away from all this Jewish business. So I went to Rome to study. I visited St. Peter's and saw the artwork. I'm a great fan of Italian literature and art. But while in Rome all I could think about was the suffering of Jews at the hands of Christians. So it wasn't so enjoyable.

A: Sort of a ruined Roman vacation.

G: Yes. I had gone to Rome to get away from the whole thing — Rome is probably the "least Jewish" place in the world. And there I was in my hotel room, thinking about — what else? — the Jews. I particularly thought about how a Jew says "*Shema Yisrael*" before giving up his life for the faith.

At this stage, I had not yet taken on any Jewish observance. But I decided to say "*Shema Yisrael*" in my hotel room by St. Peter's. When I did so, I felt an enormous surge of energy. As I was saying it, I felt that all those people who had given up their lives for Judaism were saying it with me. I felt as if I were a channel through which they were saying *Shema*. To this day, I can't explain what happened there. It was a frightening and very powerful experience.

I remember once, I went down to have breakfast. I sat down to eat, and though I was hungry, I couldn't eat. I couldn't figure out what was going on. By that time I had attended some lectures on Judaism while I had been in Israel, and so I remembered that there was one day of the year, Yom Kippur, when Jews don't eat. So I went to check the calendar, and of course, that day was Yom Kippur! I was shocked.

I had told my Jewish friends that I'd only consider converting to Judaism if I couldn't sleep at night. Well, it had come to that. I decided to convert.

A: Was that decision the hard part or the easy part?

G: I knew the road was going to be extremely difficult. Wherever I'd go in the Jewish community I'd stick out like a sore thumb, the only black guy in the room. I'm not the kind of person who likes to be in the limelight, and from now on every time I walk into a synagogue it's going to be, "Is he really an African prince?" How terrible. But I had a talk with God, and I said to Him, "Well, if that's what You want, that's it."

Sometimes a person has ups and downs in life, and he's not sure he's doing the right thing. And he often doesn't do the right thing. So at least this one thing, I was confident I'd got it right. It's a big mainstay.

A: Did you ever figure out why God played this "trick" on you — why your journey would have to be so difficult?

G: I only discovered the answer to that a few months ago. I was teaching a class on the biblical Jethro, trying to convey what kind of special person he was. And I remember what I heard many years ago from Rabbi Moshe Carlebach, who said that the first time the phrase *Baruch Hashem* ("Blessed is God") appears in the Bible is when Jethro — a convert — praises God for saving the Jews from the Egyptians.

The whole idea of a convert is that of *Baruch Hashem*, of bringing additional glory to God. That's why Jethro's Hebrew name is derived from the word *yetter*, which means "adding on." Because, as someone coming from outside the Jewish people, who is Jewish by choice, he gives additional glory to God. Not that God lacks anything, but in our eyes, we see it more.

As I was saying this in class, I heard a voice in my head saying, *Now you know why you have to go through all this — for the additional glory.* My story is not about how comfortable it is for me. It's about glorifying God. That's why I have to be so different, because only the outsider, whose Jewishness comes with great difficulty, can make this unique contribution. The big question that had been baffling and hurting me for so many years was answered.

A: But it's still hard?

G: It is, but I don't view it the same way now. It's God's world, after all, and we are His creatures. With all the fancy scenery and background, it's almost like a movie. God says to Himself: "How do you get people interested in Judaism?" So He arranges for an African prince to come around, to make people take notice and think about things. Yes, it's hard for me. But it's all about what God wants, not what I want.

ROSS HIRSCHMANN

THE KIPPAH QUANDARY

I want to make a confession: I wear a kippah. And not just in synagogue either. All the time. Even in social situations. I didn't used to. In fact, for the first 36 years of my life I only wore one in synagogue. And even that was a rarity.

The phenomenon of the switch from "no kippah" to "everyday kippah" is most indelibly recorded by the reactions you get from friends, family and coworkers. These reactions range from "Why are you

Ross Hirschmann is a former civil litigator who has been in pharmaceutical sales for the past 14 years. He earned his B.A. in history from UCLA and his J.D. from the University of California Hastings College of the Law. He lives in Los Angeles with his incredible wife and two very cute daughters.

wearing that? Is it some kind of Jewish holiday again?" to "He's such a fanatic!" to "He wears it to hide his bald spot!" (I only wish I had thought of that when my bald spot first appeared 15 years ago!)

It often starts with the polite, whispered questions. A coworker will sidle up to me, smile, move a little closer (as if he's about to confide a secret in me), look around, and then in the lowest of tones, ask the "forbidden" question. "I noticed you wear one of those, you know, thingies on your head."

"A kippah, you mean," I'll reply lightly, hoping to ease his discomfort.

"Riiight," they'll say slowly while nodding their head, "a kee-paw. So, that means you're...you know... Or-tho-dox?"

Good guess, I think to myself. You'd make a killing on "Jeopardy." I'll take Obvious Jews for $1,000. "Yes," I reply with a smile. "I'm an Orthodox Jew."

At that point the person usually leans back with a big, self-satisfied smile on his face, as if he just ate the last brownie at a family gathering. "I thought so! So, that means you, uh, can't eat a pig unless a rabbi blesses it, right?"

And it goes on from there. This is my life, ever since I decided to don my kippah.

A landmark dilemma of newfound "kippahedness" comes when confronting your first new work situation wearing the "traditional Hebraic skullcap," as one coworker deemed it. This involves meeting with someone outside your current company and thus, outside of the group who saw your slow transition from secular guy to religious guy, and who asked all the questions about your new practices and actually seemed interested in the answers. Now you are venturing beyond the safe zone, out into the final frontier.

For me, this "first contact" came while interviewing for a new job. What made it even more difficult was that it was a job I actually wanted! In other words, there was a lot at stake professionally. So now I had to make a choice. One does not have to wear a kippah to work if it will prejudice his position in a negative way. So, I had an "out" if I wanted one. But should I take the out?

To kippah or not to kippah? That was the question.

Whenever I have these deep, moral questions, I always consult my wife. She's not just smarter and cuter than I am, she's a whole lot wiser. As usual, she had a brilliantly insightful response. "Well," she said, "if you're afraid that your prospective boss may not like Jews or religious people in general, it's better to find out in the interview stage, rather than after you're working for him."

And with that, the decision was made. I would kippah.

I arrived at the interview a few minutes early and went to the men's room to check my wardrobe. I looked pretty much the same as I had in all my other job interviews. Except for the circular addition atop my head. My kippah was clean and tasteful. (I wouldn't be caught in public without a tasteful kippah!) But it was also a statement. A *big* statement. So standing there in the restroom, I hesitated for a moment and thought, "You can still take it off."

But then I realized that not wearing my kippah would be an even bigger statement. A statement of denial about who I am. A Jew. A religious Jew. So for me, going in without a kippah would be a statement that I am less-than-fully committed to those ideals around which I base my life. So, in I went — tasteful kippah and all.

The man who greeted me smiled and shook my hand. No eyes darting from my kippah to me, no jaw hanging down to the ground like in the cartoons. Just a nice "hello."

Early in the interview, he asked me, "What are you passionate about?"

"In business or in life in general?" I asked.

"Life in general," he replied.

I thought for a split second. Should I be really honest? Should I tell him what truly animates and motivates me in life? Or should I just give him the stock corporate answer that "a job well done and sacrifice for the company is what makes me tick"?

I opted for the former. I figured what the heck, he's already seen the kippah. Might as well be honest. Just go for it.

"My passions are God, family, community, and work. In that order."

I tried to soften the blow. "Probably not what a manager wants to hear! But don't misunderstand me. I work hard and take my job seriously. But it's a matter of priorities."

I looked for his response: any sign of shock or noticeable disappointment. I saw none. He simply smiled and continued the interview.

We really clicked and the rest of the interview went great. But I couldn't help wondering what he thought of my answer to that first question. At the end of the interview, he asked me if I had any questions for him.

"Just one," I said. "What are *you* passionate about in life?"

(When I later told my friends that I asked him that, they were as shocked as if I had asked him whether he wore boxers or briefs.)

"Well," he said smiling. "It's funny. As I listened to you answering that question, I felt as if I was hearing myself answer it."

I got the job shortly thereafter.

In the end, going to the interview with a kippah and answering the questions in an honest-but-not-politically-correct way, was not a heroic act. My in-laws, who survived the Nazi concentration camps; my father, who flew over 50 combat missions during World War II — they are the true heroes.

Still, what I did made a bold statement. I took a stand for something I believe in. It became clear to me that if I am only a religious Jew in private, then what, if anything, am I really? If I never take a stand on anything, then I really stand for nothing. After all, it was probably because I did stand for something that I got the job.

LAURA SINGER

GROWING UP SISTERS

My only sibling is a sister three years my senior. For as long as I can remember, we competed — in school, in social life, and most centrally with each other. Our father, himself a top competitor in sports and in business, encouraged us to compete and succeed in whatever we tried.

Like many same-sex siblings with three years between them, our childhood was fraught with rivalry and disputes. I wanted nothing more than to tag along with her, and she wanted to be the older sister, separate from me.

Jewishly, our parents let us guide our own paths.

Laura Singer is a public relations executive in Texas.

Because we were girls, the Bat Mitzvah training and celebration were made optional. I chose to do it, as school was an area in which I excelled; I saw it as another opportunity to do well and to please my parents. She chose not to, but went to a Jewish camp for two consecutive summers, and came back singing the "Grace after Meals" and more Jewishly identified than anyone in our family.

As my Bat Mitzvah drew near, she decided that she wanted one also. Her training was crammed into a year so that she, as the older sister, could experience the ceremony first. When it was my turn, I wore a dress that my mother made, at my insistence, identical to my sister's dress from the year before.

I recall my father saying to my mother, watching my sister in a circle dance at the synagogue reception, how graceful she is. I devoted myself to learning the dances so I could someday dance beside her. When she showed an interest in singing, I tried out for a singing group in college. And so it went.

During the summer before my junior year of college, my sister announced her engagement to a man she had met in college. By this point, our interactions consisted largely of lengthy letters exchanged from my college typewriter to her secretarial bay word processor — long, wordy journals of what we each were doing. My sister once commented that I was a terrible narcissist, pointing out that my letters never included the standard greeting, "How are you?" but rather launched directly into bragging about my own activities. She could always find the fault which cut me to the core.

As her wedding neared, I learned that my sister had selected a friend to be her maid of honor. I was outraged. "I'm your only sister!" I screamed over the phone. "In your whole life you'll only have one sister. I should be your maid of honor." I did not suggest that I was her closest friend, or even that my love was stronger and my loyalty greater — these reasons would never have occurred to me (and I certainly would not have picked her as my maid of honor at that time, had I given it the slightest consideration). I felt, having shared a room with her for more than a dozen years, that it was my right to stand behind her at the wedding in a brand new dress. My sister was prevailed upon, and space was made for me as "maid of honor." (The other friend, who was married, was "matron of honor." That I could live with.)

❖ ❖ ❖

I went on a trip to Israel to learn more about Judaism from an adult perspective. On the trip, I learned a section of Genesis which described the paradigmatic Jewish sisters, Rachel and Leah, who had also been pitted as erstwhile competitors. In each one's time of worst potential devastation, the other had found a way to give up something supremely meaningful to her, in order to help her sister. I found their story profoundly moving, but very remote from my own experience as a sister.

After Jacob worked for seven years to marry Rachel, Rachel learned that her father intended to bring the older sister Leah to the wedding, under a heavy veil, and marry her off to Jacob instead. It is said that Rachel and Jacob were predestined to be together and to give birth to the sons who would lead the Jewish people. Leah was predestined for another (Jacob's brother Esav), who had turned out badly, but as the oldest, tradition would have her marry first. Although Rachel and Jacob feared this switcheroo, and planned secret signs by which Jacob could confirm he had the right sister, Rachel relented and, to spare her sister the ultimate humiliation of being "spurned at the altar," shared with Leah the secret signs. And the wedding went forward.

Jacob then also married Rachel, but Leah was blessed with six sons, while Rachel remained barren for many years. One can only imagine the strain between two sisters under these circumstances, one having let her sister marry her intended, and then being forced to watch her have the children she could not.

But these are our holy ancestors, and their ways of navigating these painful circumstances establish the standard for all sisters. As the commentator Rashi explains, when Leah learned that she was again pregnant, she prayed fervently to God to make the baby a girl. Aware of the prophecy that Jacob would have 12 sons, Leah realized that her six, when added to the four sons which Jacob already had with the handmaids, would leave Rachel with a maximum of two. If Leah had a seventh son, Rachel would wind up for all eternity with only one son — that is, even fewer sons than the handmaids. Leah's prayer that her seventh baby be a girl meant that Leah was walking away from the "one-up" of all-time. The child was born a daughter.

I was overwhelmed by the self-sacrifice of these two sisters for each other, but found it very far from anything that could be said about my relationship with my own sister. I had frankly never given any thought to what she was feeling about anything.

While still in Israel, I decided to do something nice for her, and bought a silver candlestick for the baby she was expecting. Hardly on the level of giving up a son, but still a bigger gift than I had ever thought of giving before. Naturally, I felt I was being incredibly generous, and psychologically patted myself on the back. I was anxious for the baby to be born, so I could show what a nice gift I'd bought.

After his birth, I joined my sister's new "family" before sundown to bring in the baby boy's first Shabbat, and I gave her the candlestick, which she lit along with a pair that did not look like it had been getting much use. We sang *Shalom Aleichem* and welcomed the angels into her home, and then I left to go spend the rest of Shabbat with my friends.

This became a pattern that continued on Friday nights for several years. During these years, I felt very proud of myself. "She wouldn't be doing anything

Jewish at all if it weren't for me," I would tell myself. Although my sister welcomed this new tradition, and continued it even when I was not there, I felt it was all my doing. Her son's Bris was held in my home, further demonstrating my important contribution.

The nadir of our relationship was surely the Shabbat she brought her toddler son to spend with me in the Jewish community I had by that time made my home. My sister had moved 1,000 miles away six months before, and I was quite desperate to see my nephew again and to spend time with him. I had looked forward to this for months, confident that she would see my community and my observant Jewish life and acknowledge the value of my life choice.

That night, after the Shabbat evening meal, the peace dissolved. Although I thought our hosts had modeled a perfect Jewish family, with the wife's delicious and beautifully prepared food, and the husband's inspiring words of Torah, she saw it differently. "I can't believe you, of all people, would choose to live in a world which treats women as second-class citizens," she began. "If you believe that your education and life experience is worth no more than preparing a pretty dinner while your husband holds court, I guess that's your choice."

I figured I could argue her into seeing the beauty of our God-driven world, but as we repeated versions of arguments that have been made in many homes, neither convinced the other. My sister became increasingly agitated and also began to complain of a physical ailment that had plagued her for years, which I knew was exacerbated by stress. Rather than trying to tone things down, I took advantage of her discomfort to push forward. "At least my husband will be able to lead my family in a Torah discussion," I offered of my as-yet-unidentified spouse. Her pain increased, and we both kept at it.

Shabbat morning, she woke me early because her physical situation had deteriorated into great pain, and she needed a doctor. "I have two religious friends who are women and doctors who live within a block. They probably have samples of what you need that they could just give you," I offered, relishing the final twist of the knife. "But I wouldn't imagine you'd want to receive medical treatment from a second-class citizen."

As she angrily swept her still-sleeping son into her arms and headed for the door — cutting short our Shabbat together and my fantasy day with my only nephew — I did not realize how it would have been more gracious to have just run out and gotten the medicine, and skipped making the point. But our interactions were never known for delicacy or selflessness.

As I spent more time in my observant community, I was surrounded by people with stories like mine — people whose families had become distanced from them as they became more committed to living according to Torah. This struck me as a great irony, that the Torah, which teaches that we should love others as we love ourselves, and puts honoring one's parents in the Ten Commandments, should produce so much strife among family members. But, I felt, the real problem was that my sister was mistaken in not seeing the magnificence of an observant life, and thus the solution must be hers as well.

It took a trip to a spa in Costa Rica to change my view. There was a "healer in residence" who specialized in a strange practice which everyone there said could cure your life problems in one session. More as an anthropologist than a patient, I signed up. Once he had finished "curing" the problem I presented to him, he said, "There is some time left. Should we spend it on your relationship with your sister?" I was stunned. I had not mentioned anything about my family, or even that I had a sister, much less that our relationship was strained.

Even more, I had never imagined that my relationship with my sister was something which could be improved by me.

The "healer" got me thinking. Thereafter, whenever I would race around my community to do this or that act of kindness, the thought was in my head: *Would I rush to do this for my own sister?* As I swallowed a wisecrack at someone's expense at a Shabbat table, I thought, would I have swallowed that crack if I was with my family? As I handed out gifts of books of Torah wisdom to people I met in all kinds of circumstances, I wondered if perhaps my sister would also find them interesting. After all, my sister is a voracious reader. Was I a better friend and companion to everyone else than I was to my own sister?

I realized that I was scared. To act differently toward my sister was to change everything. To treat her as my special, most precious friend would make me even more vulnerable to her criticism. To recognize her Divine beauty would require me to celebrate her greatness rather than attacking her weakness. I did not know how to do that.

The Torah teaches that you love the one to whom you give. So against all odds, I started giving. Calling more often. Listening more patiently. Getting on a plane and visiting regularly. Bringing interesting books, and talking late into the night. Sending emails. Celebrating her work successes. Being her cheerleader. It got easier, and eventually, it became normal.

What I did not expect is how she reciprocated, willingly, as if she had been waiting for this door to open. A wellspring of support and big-sisterly pride came flowing back. Soon we were talking frequently, getting together for holidays. She loved me (it turns out) and relished our expanding relationship. We were well on the path toward becoming real sisters.

Meanwhile, the gap between my Torah-observance and her non-observant lifestyle was still there, just under the surface of our developing new relationship.

Years later, I watched the efforts my sister made to ensure that her son would know he was Jewish and develop a relationship with God. This concern led to her insistence that the local community strengthen its teetering Sunday School program. A community composed of largely intermarried couples, there was little parental support or knowledge to draw from. As in most cases, the person who suggests the project usually winds up with the responsibility for seeing it through, and so it was with my sister, who became the head of the Sunday School, in charge of all of its curriculum for all grades. An entire bedroom in her house was devoted to Jewish teaching materials, which she hungrily gathered from many sources and lovingly maintained for the school's future. And now my sister rides a ferry and a bus each way twice a week, so her 10-year-old can go to Hebrew school.

In some ways, the enormity of the task she had set for herself dwarfs the efforts I make to lead a Jewish life, nestled in my community with kosher markets all around and a dozen shuls within walking distance, Torah classes every night of the week and encouraging friends everywhere.

As she engrossed herself in Judaica for the school, she became more open to materials that I readily supplied from my local Jewish bookstores. She took to a particular book about Jewish marriage and studied it like a college student, flagging pages, underlining passages and quoting from it in conversation. I sent others, including *How to Get Your Prayers Answered* by Rabbi Irwin Katsof, and *The Bible for the Clueless but Curious* by Rabbi Nachum Braverman. She devoured them. Another commonality was born.

At some point, having an only child became unbearable for her, but she and her husband found themselves with "secondary infertility," a not uncommon phenomenon where a fertile couple finds that they do not produce a second child. My sister suffered greatly over this, complaining tearfully that "there is a hole in my family where another child is supposed to be" and seeing every woman with a baby while she had none.

Heartbroken, they prepared to adopt and/or foster one or more children, reconfiguring their entire house for the anticipated child (as required by foster care regulations), advertising for adoptions, and using every resource to pursue leads. I found her endless misery exhausting, but tried to be supportive by listening and by contributing to the project financially. (It finally occurred to me that charity begins at home.)

Eventually, they were blessed with the adoption of a healthy baby boy. My sister then explained how it really happened. She had read a teaching by Rebbe Nachman of Breslov: "Pour your heart out to God in the forest." My sister had figured that since she lived near a national forest, she should do just that. She had, for 40 consecutive days, trudged out to the forest — rain or shine — and prayed until she wept. It was shortly after that effort concluded, without missing a day, and sometimes in the dark, that she located a young woman whose unborn child would become my sister's second son.

My sister prayed by herself in the forest until she wept, for 40 days. I don't know if I have wept a total of 40 times during prayer over the past decade.

More than a year after the adoption, my sister called me, sounding very dark. "I had a miscarriage," she said quietly. "It's been very painful, and very confusing," she said, as one would only imagine after shedding so many tears and being told so many times that it was impossible for her to get pregnant at all. "I'm not telling Mom and Dad," she said.

In the weeks before the miscarriage, they had felt that maybe God was rewarding them for adopting a son. They were devastated by the loss. "But," she added, "I thought you would want to know."

In her most painful moment, my sister was able to transcend her pain to convey what was, in a way, wonderful news for me. Her supposed "infertility" over the past years had weighed heavily on my spirit. As she well knew, my health had always tracked hers. Three years after she developed asthma, I had also; her stomach problems presaged similar ones for me. Her "infertility" in her 30s had been sad for her as the mother of one, but for me it was devastating, threatening to end my hopes of ever conceiving.

So, my dear sister wanted me to know that she could still conceive — so I could, too.

"I know this was hard for you," I told her later. Then I told her the story of Rachel and Leah, of absorbing a loss to give a sister joy. "I feel I have a sister," I said.

110

"I feel that, too," she said. "I remember the day they brought you home from the hospital," she shared with me for the first time.

"I always thought you were annoyed that I entered your world," I said.

"Are you kidding?" she laughed. "I was so excited, I loved you immediately."

I never knew.

RICHARD RABKIN

MY TEAM

W hen I was eight years old I decided that the San Francisco 49ers were *my* football team. On a trip to San Francisco, my family and I paid a visit to the 49ers' home stadium, Candlestick Park. I saw the giant posters of quarterback Joe Montana and star receiver Jerry Rice, and the jersey of high-stepping running back Roger Craig. As a young Jewish boy from Canada, the strongest person I had ever met was my gym/computer science teacher Fred Cohen. So to me, these men were giants. In an instant, they became my idols, and this team became *my team*.

I began to follow the San Francisco 49ers with vigor. Every Sunday or Monday they played, the TV

Richard Rabkin is a lawyer living in Toronto. He is the editor of Jewlarious.com.

was off limits to anyone who wasn't wearing red and white, and if you even thought about picking up the remote control you would be the recipient of a blindside tackle by a little Ronnie Lott in training — even if you were my sister (sorry, Jessica).

Every win wasn't just a win for the 49ers; it was a win for me.

As the years went on, my sense of being part of the team grew to the point where I felt that my actions could somehow influence the 49ers' success. If I wasn't able to watch the whole game and the 'Niners lost, it was probably because I hadn't been watching. If a friend had called and the opposing team scored a touchdown, then this friend was obviously cursed and henceforth banned from calling during game play.

I even had the strange ritual of eating a frosted malt after the third quarter and chewing on the little wooden spoon for the first few minutes of the fourth. If I didn't, I thought the coach would call Joe Montana over and tell him, "That Canadian guy didn't chew his wooden spoon today. Put the football down. We're leaving."

Even though it sounds crazy — alarmingly crazy — the proof was in the pudding (or in the frosted malt). The San Francisco 49ers won four Super Bowls in the 1980s and 13 division titles in the '80s and '90s combined. We were practically unstoppable.

Our streak came to an abrupt end in 1994 when I went off to college and kind of lost interest in football, which just so happens to be the very same year that the 49ers won their last Super Bowl. (If you think that's just a coincidence, you've obviously never had a frosted malt before.) I still enjoyed football, but I just didn't feel like a 49er anymore.

Around the same time, I went off to Israel and got reacquainted with my Jewish roots. The more I studied and grew in my relationship with Judaism, the more I realized that I was already a member of a team, a very holy team. I called it: Team Jew.

I realized that my intense relationship with the San Francisco 49ers had actually taught me how to feel a part of the Jewish people. Just as I felt I had personally won when the 49ers had a victory, when I heard about an Israeli rescue team digging out some survivors in Africa, or about a Jew doing some act of kindness and performing a *kiddush Hashem* (a sanctification of God's name), I felt as though their actions were a victory for me, too, because they were on my team.

I also realized that my actions, no matter how seemingly insignificant, could have an impact on my team. If I carried out an act of kindness, it could inspire someone else to do the same. If I performed a mitzvah like learning Torah, the spiritual ripples generated could have a powerful effect on a team member halfway across the world.

Observing these commandments didn't taste as chocolaty as a frosted malt, but their impact on my team was far more genuine and everlasting.

YAACOV DEYO

THE PERFECT STORM

S o what about Albert Schweitzer?! Is he going to go to hell, too?!"

I never really knew much about Albert Schweitzer, except that he was a good guy, a doctor who went to Africa and won the Nobel Peace Prize in the '50s. I also knew that if I brought up his name now, this religious-type guy I was talking to in Harvard Square was toast.

The tall man with the thin tie and upbeat Southern accent looked a little deflated. In my gut I felt sorry because he looked a little hurt, too. He wanted to reach

Yaacov Deyo is a graduate of Harvard College, where he studied physics and economics. He received his rabbinic degree from Aish HaTorah in 1996. He is a founder of SpeedDating and Jewish Impact Films, and is presently the managing director of the Jewish Enrichment Center in Manhattan.

out to me, and I was having fun with him.

"Yes," the man said, "Albert Schweitzer is going hell for not believing in the Lord."

"Well that's unacceptable," I replied. He seemed to expect that answer, having, I would imagine, a lot of conversations with the same flow.

The rest of freshman year didn't do much more for my beliefs. I was summed up as a nice kid on the rowing team who knows a lot of physics and gave up Catholicism for Lent. Even after I quoted Trotsky and Kant, my mother wasn't very happy about the last bit — leaving Catholicism. She expected me to follow my own path, and imagined I might even become a Republican. In the end it was converting to Judaism and becoming an Orthodox rabbi that kind of threw her for a loop.

Soon after freshman year I started putting my own religion together. It wasn't that I wanted to get listed as a new prophet; it was more to find a respite from classes at Harvard. The cathedral in Cambridge was great because the boys' choir of Boston studied there. On Sunday mornings it was beautiful to hear the voices. Sometimes as it snowed I'd sit there and wish I could go sing with them in the way I used to sing when I was an altar boy. I couldn't sing now, though; I had given up a belief in God. It wouldn't be right to get up there and sing if I didn't believe the words. The whole organized religion thing did not make sense to me. So as with many of my peers, I put together a patchwork of religious icons and experiences.

After my cathedral phase, I moved on to Tai Chi. Master Quong taught a class where I learned how to grasp the pheasant's tail. I got into foreign movies and saw a lot of Hong Kong cinema.

I was drawn toward activism. I took Robert Cole's class, *The Literature of Social Reflection.* Flannery O'Conner, William Carlos Williams, James Agee, stories about Gandhi. This class convinced me not to go to Wall Street.

Indiana Jones influenced that decision, too. Retro clothes, leather satchels, c'mon! — a white horse, going on a quest without killing people, and the cool whip in an Arabian bazaar! I checked to see if Harvard offered a class in whips. In the end, the closest thing offered was knife throwing. Did Emile Zola throw knives? I didn't think so. That's when I started to think maybe I would try and change the world.

During summer vacations I learned how to build boats on Martha's Vineyard where my family spent our summers. I met a guy there, a designer who built ocean-racing wooden trimarans. He needed someone to help build these boats made almost entirely out of wood. He hired me on a trial to learn the skill. French people would show up at his workshop and show him pictures of spaceship-like crafts flying through the water. These were his own designs. Cool! After four summers working for him, I picked up a decent carpenter's skill.

It was that fourth summer that I first saw *Rogue Wave.*

She lay nearly 60 feet along the water line, and perhaps six feet above it tops, making her look like something out of *Star Wars*. With her three pearl white parallel hulls she had a 25-foot beam. Did someone say strong presence? Think Concorde's cousin who went to sea and did very well, thank you. Rising from her main deck shot a mast shaped like an airplane wing, giving her 140 square feet of windage *before* she unfurled her canvas. For all her power, this was a swan in flight. Taking her out of dockage, and then bringing her around for a beam reach, she would buck forward until you had to *hold on* she accelerated so fast. She could do 30 knots on a good clean sea, and do it with nothing but the wind. I was in love, and I had found my white horse.

All that summer we sailed her around Vineyard Sound. I gave her epoxy and red cedar, and she gave me a sparkle in the eye I still see in the mirror today.

So when a wealthy British-type guy came to buy her, my heart raced when he mentioned he would need to take delivery in Dubai, the Emirates. Holy! He asked if my boss knew anyone who could sail her over to Europe, through the Med (*Ulysses*, wine-colored seas — I'm there!), down the Red Sea (as in Moses!), into the Gulf of Sudan, and then through the Strait of Hormuz (excuse me, Iran-Iraq War), and then home inside the Arabian Peninsula.

I was thrilled at the opportunity.

I raised my hand.

As it turned out, I didn't get the chance to take her

across the Atlantic. Something better came along.

My sister Catherine had a friend who had done a paper on a non-violent movement in Northern Ireland that had raised quite a stir. What if I went over and checked it out? I figured if I wanted to change the world, I had to see what worked and what didn't. I could meet up with the rest of *Rogue*'s crew in Spain, and then take her on to Dubai. We would get to the Mideast in June, leaving extra time to go to Nicaragua for research before school started again in the fall. It sounded like a plan.

So after three years in Cambridge, I took the year off and flew to Belfast. I got involved with groups who did conflict resolution projects. One in particular brought Catholic and Protestant children from the city out into the countryside together to farm and do sports. It didn't seem to work so well. Once the kids returned to their environments, the animosity and ignorance came right back.

I met with lots of Catholics and Protestants. Many took an interest in trying to bring me back into believing again. I was a lot nicer than I was with Mr. Southern Accent, but I still didn't get it. I went on different retreats, read neat intellectual Christian journals, and basically did more due diligence. But I couldn't reconcile concepts like "killing a god" and the previously unscheduled Second Coming.

My mother explained that the logic of it was that you had to suspend logic, a supra-logic which understands the limits of our logic. I reread Aquinas and St.

Augustine during long hikes around Belfast, and in the end gave it a rest; it did not seem reasonable to me to forgo reason before its time. It seemed like there was a lot more going on in cosmology. So I moved to that for my spiritual questing for a while.

I met up with the boat crew in Spain, and *Rogue Wave* was ready to sail in early spring. Repairs had been made to her mast, and the last of the stores were aboard. The owner came to visit, took us out to dinner, gave us each gifts of books and checked on the armaments. Since *Rogue Wave* would be sailing in the Indian Ocean, she had to have some defense against piracy. And heading for a Muslim country with guns on board seemed like the prudent thing to do. We carried semi-automatic rifles and shotguns with hollow point shells designed to pierce a boarder's hull right below the waterline.

I called my mom and she asked if I had my Irish knit sweater. (I didn't.) She told me how back in Ireland the fishermen would each have a distinct pattern of cabling on their sweaters, so when their bloated, disfigured bodies washed ashore, the families could identify them. I thanked her for the information. With that we set sail for the first leg, a 600-mile trip to Sidi Bu Said, a port just outside Tunis, Tunisia.

I never imagined that my white horse would lead me to God, but she did.

Two days out from Almeria we got caught in a brewing gale driving in from the west. With hundreds of miles of sea as pitch, 30- and 40-foot waves began to form. The barometer fell. I started throwing up. The winds grew even stronger, and I threw up some more. After 10 hours it was getting dark and I got off watch; the seas had climbed to 50 feet and the winds to 60 knots (about 70 mph). By then I had thrown up everything I had ever eaten.

Two hours later, the captain called me to come back up on watch. Being an old WWII veteran fighter pilot, he was a real stalwart who usually woke me for watch by gently squeezing my arm while reciting Beatnik poetry. Not this time. Up on deck things had gotten a lot worse.

Coming up from below I turned first toward the bow and saw something I will never forget. A black wall of water a couple of hundred feet in front of us rose upward as far as I could see, becoming lost in a most angry mass of clouds and rain. I couldn't tell water from wind; it was all one. It was like Godzilla had become a tower of water and was looking down on us.

The captain gave me the helm and went below to wake the other two fellows. We had taken all the sails down, but with *Rogue*'s airplane-foil mast she was still doing 15 knots. We had no sail flying and we were going 15 knots.

Alone on deck, I tried to get my bearings. The howling scream of the wind made it so I couldn't hear my own voice even while shouting. *Rogue Wave* was working the storm with all her strength, twisting and shuddering. I could feel it through my feet. I burst

121

into tears as I felt her main wood beams groaning. Poor *Rogue*! I knew those beams, and here they were being tormented. The beautiful lines of her hull were lost in the darkness, leaving only her sounds of torment.

Then I began to notice a rhythm. *Rogue Wave* rose on the front of the waves coming from behind us, and we shot upwards a nearly level keel of seven stories in under six seconds. Near the top of the wave we arched forward and began surfing downward, forward and fast, crashing into the trough. The wave would find us again and raise us up its forward side, and down once more we would surf. Sometimes the movement ended when the giant wave passed underneath us, despite our speed, leaving us to fall off its back, down again into the trough, disheveled, slightly canted, and waiting for the next temporary ride.

It was a force nine gale, a tad below a hurricane, and *Rogue Wave* was in a grand and powerful waltz. My terror faded as I anticipated the boat's moves. My concerns for the boat faded as well. She was enjoying this as I might a hard, hard workout.

I looked around to each side, trying to see more, feel more. As I did, my relationship to the storm changed further still. Taking a deep breath of air, I tasted the clear, clean fresh water of the rain. It was slightly chilled! I laughed, breathed in deeper, licked the rain from my lips, and started to feel strong. As I made steerage I started hearing Schiller's poem in the choral of Beethoven's ninth. Crash! Water exploded off the bow as *Rogue* hurtled herself deep into the forward wave. If *Rogue* could waltz, then I could breathe and feel strong, too.

With a full heart and the happiest of eyes, I shouted, "Hey storm! We are brothers, you and I!"

It was at that moment that I felt my voice mouth the words, "Oh my God." In that briefest instant, at a deep, intuitive level, I was forever changed.

It took me another few moments to articulate my intuitive perception. I realized that the storm could be by chance (through the laws of quantum mechanics), and my own evolutionary existence could be by chance. But my relationship to the storm — one of terror, awe, admiration, sublime fear, and love — that relationship could not be the result of any chance-driven mechanism.

There was no way two unconnected products of vastly different chaos-driven mechanisms could have such an elegant, powerful and symbiotic relationship. Rather it was an expression of God, and I was feeling the unity of existence. God had sent me a letter and had used half of the Mediterranean as stationary.

The rest of the crew came on deck, and we began deploying sea anchors. There was a fear that the whole boat would flip upside down and capsize.

I thanked God for this second communique, of irony and intimacy, because in every sense, He had just capsized my own world.

Fantastic energy and rose petal softness at the

same time. God cares about me. I smiled deep in my heart, helped put out the sea anchors, and then threw up some more. Life continues, even after epiphanies. But now, there's no turning back.

YAEL MERMELSTEIN

COMING TO TERMS

I grew up thinking that life was supposed to follow a certain pattern. You reach a certain age and you get married, then the kids come. Each one is carried for nine months and born into a world that is deliriously happy to see him, where they grow up with the balanced parenting of two harmonious partners.

Although I seem to have been somewhat mistaken in my rosy perception of the universe, I also discovered that some of these wonderful things *do* happen to some people. But it is rare to find a person for whom *all* of these things go smoothly.

That is why I did not feel bitterness that cold November, when I found myself laid up in the

Yael Mermelstein holds an M.A. in Jewish education, and teaches at a post-high school institution in Israel. She publishes regularly for children and for adults. She lives in Beitar Illit with her husband and children.

hospital with premature contractions, expecting child number two. Child number one had arrived in the seventh month, and the doctors were just a wee bit nervous about the outcome of this one.

My roommate was a woman who had been through the long struggle of infertility, and now that she was finally full with new life, the doctors weren't taking any chances.

We struck up a fast and tender friendship as often happens in these situations. We were at exactly the same stage of the game. We lay there together each morning, strapped with monitor belts, listening to the steady "thump, thump" of our unborn children. We fell in love with the signs of life within us. There was a palpable sense that there were four of us in that room.

At the end of the week, we were both discharged to continue our hibernation in our respective homes. We exchanged phone numbers.

As we lay in our homes, whiling away the empty hours of bed rest, we called each other with updates.

"We passed the 30-week mark — can you believe it!"

"We made it to 31. Our babies have a fighting chance of making it to term!"

"Thirty-two weeks! They're bigger than three pounds!" Things were really looking up.

We never had the 33-week conversation. My baby was already out and fighting for every breath by then.

The phone rang. It was *her*.

"Tell her I can't come to the phone," I told my husband. It was true. I couldn't come to the phone to hear about her baby, kicking and growing inside her protected womb, while mine lay minuscule and helpless in the neonatal unit.

I bumped into her in the hospital; she was there for a routine visit. She saw me carrying a bottle of milk.

"You had the baby!" She was exuberant. And then, "I tried calling so many times." I gave her a weak smile.

"It's hard," I said. I looked at her swollen middle enviously.

"I understand." She looked at me with genuine sympathy, and I felt genuinely sorry for myself.

That night, I tossed about in bed. Conflicting emotions raged within me.

Do you not believe that God, in His infinite wisdom, doles out to each what they can handle? Don't you know that this is the test that was crafted just for you?

And then, *You already have a child. Stop with the righteous indignation. You are not entitled to anything in this world. Everything is a gift.*

And yet, I found no peace.

My feelings ballooned to include all fertile women who were able to carry a baby for nine full months. They had earned a token badge of womanhood that I was never to wear. Every friend who delivered on time was a threat to my sense of self-worth, and it marred my ability to be happy for them.

"Envy, greed and pursuit of honor take a person out of this world" (Talmud, Avot 4:28). Was I not guilty of all three of these vices? I felt the truth behind these words — I had removed myself from my life as I knew it, and I was moving into an acrid-tasting territory.

A few weeks later, I was in the hospital delivering milk to my baby. I saw her there again. She was with another woman, perhaps her labor coach. *She must be due about now,* I surmised.

She walked up to me and looked at me, her eyes were strong and clear. In a firm voice she told me, "I have to be strong. It's all over."

My heart shattered into a thousand shards of pain, as she subtly informed me that she was about to deliver a stillborn child.

If you could have seen the maternity ward that day, you would have seen two women embracing. One had a child in the neo-natal unit, reaching and grasping for new life each day. Her guilt found respite in the tears that coursed down her cheeks. The other was accepting the profound loss of what would never be.

And the master plan for me became clear.

From that day forward, my heart became clean of envy, greed and the need for honor in regard to this issue. I did not beg for the lot of others, only for what was meant for me. Seeing the blessing of a child who survived, I was more than amply grateful for my portion. Having the great merit to bear children at all was honor enough. I did not want for more.

The equanimity with which my friend accepted her loss created a stirring within me that I will never forget. She was grateful to have had the chance to carry a child, and that brought her some measure of solace. She was a bulwark of faith in the face of adversity.

"We will find the message in this," she said.

Any strength of character that resulted from the experience was drawn from her well and poured into mine. And for that I am forever grateful.

A few years later I heard through the grapevine that she had given birth to twins. I had just given birth to my third premature baby. I called her up, and hearing her voice, a delight so pure and real flowed through me. I knew beyond a shadow of a doubt that this time, my tears — tears of joy — were for her, and her alone.

LOOKING FOR MR. MUNK

Like most young Jewish boys growing up in Toronto, I began to attend Hebrew school at about the age of seven. Hebrew school at the local synagogue was two hours each day after public school from Monday through Thursday, and two hours on Sunday mornings. I cannot tell you the number of great street hockey games that were abruptly ended with, "Harvey, get ready for Hebrew school."

Being the youngest of four boys, with only six years between my oldest brother and myself, I was already primed for the Hebrew school experience that

Rabbi Tzvi Nightingale is the executive director of Aish South Florida.

awaited me. I had heard from my brothers about the horror stories, the boredom, the teachers with funny accents and the gum-stuck desks. I had endured many years of "I hate Hebrew school and I'm not going back" from Reuben and Sid. Yes, Hebrew school was something I was really looking forward to.

I remember the first day like it was yesterday. I can still recall the walk from my father's car in the parking lot to the school entrance, the same walk a prisoner must experience as he begins serving his sentence. My sentence was to last until my Bar Mitzvah.

We met the principal, Mr. Frank,* a short bald man with beady eyes and a mole on his left cheek. A sinister smile came over his lips as I was passed over to his mentorship. I was placed in Mrs. Kahanavitch's class. When it came my turn to read, not ever seeing a word of Hebrew, I looked down at the script which just as well could have been Chinese and promptly broke into tears. This reaction elicited a return visit by Mr. Frank, who now put me into Mr. Goodman's class, which was, in my mind, the class for dummies. I stayed there until I somehow was placed into Mr. Ogman's grade one class.

I endured the deathly, daily ritual of learning to read Hebrew. We were expected to fight boredom and always know the spot in order to be able, at any time, to answer the most oft-asked question in the class, "Nightingale, where are we?" And Heaven help you if you did

---

* All the names, other than Mr. Munk's, have been changed.

not know the place. Then you would be subjected to the corporal punishment of Mr. Ogman's yellow stick; an act that would land him in jail and slap him with a lawsuit if he were to use it on a kid today.

My greatest achievement in that first grade came one Sunday morning before Mr. Ogman arrived. I went to the cupboard where he kept that feared yellow stick and tossed it out of the second-story window into the snowy alleyway below, where it was immediately buried in a white coffin of powder, never to be seen again. The look of confusion when he went to retrieve his weapon is something I still cherish. Even more special was the loyalty the class exhibited when he asked where it was — not one person, not even the goody-goody, said a word.

In second grade, I was put into Mr. Jacobson's class. Mr. Jacobson was a sweet, short man who had no control over the kids. He was the opposite of Mr. Ogman. The charade in Mr. Jacobson's class was the request to use the bathroom. *"Ani rotzeh latzeit"* — I wish to go out [to the bathroom] — was the only Hebrew sentence that every little Jewish child was adept at. It was your ticket to a short reprieve from the sheer boredom where you could wander the halls for the most allowable time that could be construed as really taking care of your needs.

And then came grade three, taught by the dreaded Mr. Munk. I had heard the stories of Mr. Munk from my brothers. He was stern. He would take no guff (that's what we used to say in those days) from anyone. Step out of line in Mr. Munk's class and he plays piano on your fingers. Whereas Mr. Ogman was reviled and Mr. Jacobson almost pitied, Mr. Munk was feared.

And this is when everything about Hebrew school changed. Mr. Munk was feared all right. He was tall, had a German accent, gold teeth that glistened when he spoke, was very proud and stood erect. But there was something different. In Mr. Munk's class Judaism was not a bore. He taught with passion, love and intensity. He did not teach like he was a caretaker of misbehaving kids in a zoo for two hours. He taught like he was going to make an impression on us. And impress he did.

I came to love and look forward to his classes. I can still hear him tell us that if the Almighty could redeem the Jewish people from Egypt, did we really have to fear the Egyptian armies? I remember learning the Book of Joshua, and even recall him teaching us Rashi. I remember how proud I felt when I was awarded for going to synagogue or knowing the most answers of an assignment. I still can sing the songs he taught us from Hallel, songs that he said the Israeli soldiers used to sing as they prepared for battle.

Mr. Munk loved being Jewish, was proud of being Jewish, and conveyed that love and pride. He became my first true rebbe. Because of him I began to go to shul every week.

This took place when I was 11. I continued attending synagogue well after my Bar Mitzvah. When

I was 15, I started to read novels by Chaim Potok, and that inspired me even more to learn about Judaism. Potok painted a picture of learning Torah and living a Jewish life that I knew all my grandparents were keenly aware of, but that I had missed out on.

For a hundred generations Jews had lived the way Potok was describing and I was not about to let it end with me. I began attending an Orthodox shul and ended up meeting a high school student who invited me to learn at Ner Yisrael Yeshiva in Toronto. There I hooked up with a couple of young rabbis who taught me, until I heard of Aish HaTorah in Jerusalem, where I studied from the summer of '79, received rabbinic ordination, and ended up in Florida where I am presently the director of Aish South Florida.

Over the years it had crossed my mind to try to contact Mr. Munk and tell him what had become of me. I had no idea where he might be, or even if he was still alive. I never really followed through, however, until one day I picked up a book translated by an Eliyahu Munk. I read the back flap about the translator, and it mentioned that he was living in Israel and had been an educator in Toronto for many years. I was not sure if it was the same man; I never knew his first name — he was always just Mr. Munk.

I still did not pursue it, until one day, about four months ago, one of my students said that I really should try to track him down. So I went to the obvious source to begin an investigation — Google. I googled Mr. Munk, found the Eliyahu Munk that did the translations and even found an email address for him at his publishing house. I emailed and got a reply back that they would forward my message to Eliyahu Munk.

A few weeks later I received the following email:

Dear Rabbi Nightingale,

I was thrilled to hear from you. I am indeed the person you were looking for. During the past 25 years I have been a resident of Jerusalem with my wife. We have been blessed with 20 grandchildren and 15 great-grandchildren. Needless to add that these, as well as our four children, are all in Israel. We just celebrated our 60th anniversary surrounded by them all.

My "literary" career began when I made aliyah, one of the motives being to spread Torah to a larger audience than merely a classroom of children who did not really look for Torah in the first place in their after-public-school hours. I'd love to hear more about you, or better still meet you again on your next trip to Israel.

Sincerely, Eliyahu Munk

I immediately emailed him back and told him what had become of me, and the impact that he had had on my life choices and career. He was quite pleased and said that it had made his day, nay his week. He informed me that in January, he would be in Miami for a few weeks.

❖　❖　❖

I pulled up to the Best Western Hotel in Surfside

and climbed the steps of the '60s-style, bright yellow motel that had not yet met with a wrecking ball for a high-rise like those being built around it all over North Beach. Outside of room 426 an elderly lady sat reading in the sun. I approached, but before I said a word, she looked up at me and said, "Rabbi Nightingale?"

"Yes, and you must be Mrs. Munk."

She led me into the motel room, and Mr. Munk came out looking quite casual in his three-button shirt. After 33 years, Mr. Munk was not so tall, not so imposing, and not so stern. We chatted and exchanged family pictures. We went to lunch at a nearby café and talked some more. I told him what I was doing, the types of programs Aish runs, how we conduct the Shabbat learner service, and about other innovations Aish has created in Jewish education. We talked about the old Hebrew school, how long he had been there, and his teaching career in Israel the past number of years and of his writings and classes.

The conversation turned to Torah, and Mr. Munk began to cite Jewish law, quoting medieval commentaries and verses of Torah. He gave his insights and novel understandings of all kinds of things, including the Sin of the Golden Calf.

As I sat there listening to him, a strange thing happened. His words faded into the background. Time had stopped and began retreating backwards. There it was again. His passion, his love, his pride — of Torah, of Judaism, of being Jewish. There it was once again in front of my eyes. That same energy that he had when he stood in front of our grade three class on those cold winter afternoons in Toronto was there again in front of me, 33 years later, in a café in sunny Miami Beach. His face again lit up, his piercing eyes, his mouth curling with words of Torah — it was all identical to those days in Hebrew school so long ago. And I sat, once again, enraptured by it.

His wife indicated that maybe he was going on too long but I said, "No, no, don't you see...?"

I could not hold back the tears. It was too over-whelming...to be a 10-year-old boy and a 43-year-old man all at the same moment.

We left the café, walked back to the motel and said our goodbyes. I told them I would bring my family by on the Sunday before they left, which I did. Before we had gone to lunch they gave me a gift that I put in my car. I opened it after I had pulled away from the motel. It was a pretty glass and metal artwork with *Birkat HaBayit* — the Blessing for the Home.

Was the gift intentional? Didn't he already know that he had given me that gift? Were it not for Mr. Munk, I would not have the Jewish home I have today. A home with my wife and six children; keeping Shabbat, keeping kosher, talking about the weekly Torah portion with the kids' parsha sheets. A home with weekly Shabbat guests that have never or seldom experienced the beauty and wisdom of being Jewish. A home where I try to pass on the love and passion for Judaism to others, the way that Mr. Munk passed it on to me.

DR. JACKIE YARIS

MURMURS IN THE DARK

A few months ago near my office, I noticed a partially blind man walking along the street. I began to see him daily, his cane tapping the way in front of my building, and I watched as he tried to approach passersby with his lopsided smile and cloudy eyes. Each day I would cringe as, almost invariably, they would look away, cross the street or create a wide arc to avoid him.

When he was able to ensnare someone, he got a little too close, spoke with his somewhat garbled voice a little too loud, and his head jerked up and down

---

Dr. Jackie Yaris is a physician practicing internal medicine in Beverly Hills, CA. She is also a wife and the mother of three young children.

excitedly as they smiled gamely, looked aside and left as soon as they could. As person after person left him with his cane and broad grin, I watched as he stood abandoned in the middle of the bustling sidewalk, and ached for how isolated he must feel.

It saddened me that his obvious disability created an almost physical barrier. What I have realized though, in my 10 years of practicing medicine, is that loneliness is not merely the affliction of the disabled. It is far more pervasive.

Numerous times I am confronted by patients seeking not only medical advice, but something far more difficult for mc to give.

A few weeks ago, I was called at 10 p.m. by a woman in her 80s. She was concerned about how to take her medicine the next day so as not to burden her grandson who was taking her on a special outing. We planned a strategy and got off the phone. At midnight she called and reiterated the times she was to take her medicine.

Wearily I mumbled, "Uh, huh...sounds right... good night."

But I had heard it. The desperation. After years of these late-night phone calls, I have learned to recognize it in the lingering at the end of sentences, or the longing desire to engage me in conversation.

"My grandson...he's a good boy," she ventured.

Trying hard to sleep and talk simultaneously, I whispered, "Yeah, he sounds great...goodnight... sleep well." A few more minutes of that and I was finally able to get off the phone.

At 2 a.m. when she called, my husband groaned and got up to find a quieter place to sleep. She again needed to review her medicines, but I could hear the fear in her thin voice. Though I was exhausted, I knew she hadn't called about her medicine. She had paged me because the night was cold and long, and she was alone. I could almost feel her clinging to my words, so I stayed on the phone awhile and hoped that my groggy, disjointed murmurs in the dark offered her some relief.

As their worlds diminish by deaths or illness, many old people are left by themselves, but it is not only because of their failing bodies.

One of my patients in her mid-70s, whom I hadn't seen in a year, came in for an exam. A cancer survivor, I remembered her as a spunky, no-nonsense woman, a firestorm with wrinkles and white hair, who, despite being hunched over with osteoporosis, traveled the world. I noticed a distinct difference this year — her thinning hair was put up in a jaunty clip and a bright lipstick covered her cracked lips.

"Okay, Dr. Yaris...don't laugh." I raised one eyebrow in question. "I did it... I got plastic surgery."

That was the difference. She showed me where the surgeon had taken fat from her abdomen and injected it into her face to make "cheek bones."

"But the fat is slipping toward my ears..."

I was surprised. The year before she had seemed the type to scoff at such frivolity, but she continued. "I was

140

in Egypt and had this tour guide...so handsome... you know what I mean..." She pursed her lips conspiratorially. "It's just that...it's just that..." This is when her voice became small and hesitant. "He didn't see me. I chatted and joked, but he just didn't see..."

She lowered her eyes so I wouldn't see they were wet. "I may look like this, but I still feel like I'm 25... and now I have fat ears..." She sighed and tried to smile, but I could see the despair.

I began to recognize how lonely it must be to be so marginalized and misunderstood in a youth-oriented society. Since then, when I see the aged, their bright eyes forced downward by necks contorted with arthritis or imprisoned by wooden faces immobilized by strokes, occasionally being pushed by foreigners speaking into cell phones, I seek out their eyes to let them know that I see.

I once thought that loneliness is solely the purview of the aging in a culture that doesn't treasure its old, but my years of practice have taught me otherwise.

Frequent moves, long work hours and fewer family relationships isolate the younger, too. One of my patients — a beautiful singer-songwriter who just released her first CD — called me at 5:30 a.m., begging to get an early morning appointment. When she came in, her hair pulled back and dark glasses on, she slumped and absently fidgeted with her scarf.

"I'm so sorry to have called you so early this morning. I waited as long as I could." She pulled off her glasses and her eyes were red and swollen.

I looked at her grayish face and thin lips and recalled the cover of her CD where she stood sparkling, poised and confident, and was shocked at the change.

"It was a hard night." She was staying at the Beverly Hills Hotel because her house was being fumigated. "I don't know what happened," she said, "but suddenly I felt this sense of dread and my heart started racing, and I felt like I couldn't breathe."

I saw that she was winding and unwinding her scarf tightly through her manicured fingers. "I tried to relax, but my heart kept pounding. I didn't know what to do." She was breathing shallowly. "It was horrible... I thought I was going to die..." Her breath wheezed through clenched teeth. "I wanted to call 911, but I felt so stupid. Instead I called room service because I didn't want to die alone."

She looked up at me unblinking and pinched her palm with her nails. "I thought I was going to die," she whispered and shuddered. "I hugged tightly to my stuffed Dumbo, curled up on the bed, and finally at about 2 a.m. I slept a little." She shook her head. "I never want to go through anything like that again."

A full work-up revealed that she most likely had a classic panic attack. But it is the image of that stunning young woman alone in the middle of one of the most expensive, opulent hotels in the world, shaking uncontrollably and clutching a stuffed elephant, that stays with me.

142

I have come to learn that loneliness is a universal problem. And while people don't offer their loneliness up very readily, I hear it. I hear it in the echoes of what they say. In the hush of unfinished answers when I ask about spouses and kids, and in the void when I question about support systems and social networks. It hovers at the edge of late-night phone calls and lives in the silences.

But in the era of cell phones, emails, BlackBerries and BlueBerries, when people are able to be connected now more than ever before, why are so many so alone?

I don't know, but something I saw the other day gives me hope.

It was the blind man. But this time he was not alone. Close to him was a woman with a slightly misshapen forehead, milky eyes and unmatched clothing. I watched, that bleak December morning, as they leaned forward and spoke to each other with garbled voices — a little too loud, and a little too close. A few minutes later, the blind man was exclaiming so excitedly that his head started to rock back and forth. As if by instinct, the woman linked her arm through his and she too began to rock.

My throat caught as I watched the two of them sitting at the bus stop, canes propped to the side, heads bobbing up and down in unison, huddled together against the cold. A piece of loneliness had been washed away.

RABBI YAAKOV SALOMON

A FACE IN THE WINDOW

June. Ah... June. Tulips. Suntan lotion. Baseball. Graduations. Barbeques. Finals (finally). Summer camp. Really red watermelon. Sunglasses. Father's Day.

What a month, indeed. Someday, when they ask me to recalibrate the calendar, I'm going to lop off a good eight to ten days from each of December, January and February and add them to June. No

Rabbi Yaakov Salomon, C.S.W. is a noted psychotherapist, in private practice in Brooklyn, NY for over 25 years. He is a senior lecturer and the creative director of Aish HaTorah's Discovery Productions. He is also an editor and author for the ArtScroll Publishing Series, and a featured writer on Aish.com. Rabbi Salomon shares his life with his wife, Temmy, and their unpredictable family.

reason why the greatest month of the year shouldn't have 60 or 70 days, at least!

Until then, 30 will just have to do. Oh well.

But for me, June always had an additional significance. It contained my father's birthday. Not that he ever made much of it (and, in typical European fashion, we never knew how old he was), but it did add a dash of supplementary luster to an already celebratory time of year.

Come to think of it, Daddy never made much of Father's Day, either. And since his birthday and Father's Day inevitably fell so close to each other, my brother and I usually cheated and rolled the festivities into one. Daddy just kind of smiled approvingly at our annual shortcut, perhaps gladdened that less of a fuss would be made over him. In fact, if I didn't know better, and if he hadn't been born in Poland, I'd have suspected that he orchestrated his own birth to land in the vicinity of Father's Day, precisely to escape some additional rays of limelight. He was reticent and unassuming. (Nothing like his son.)

I wonder if he was always unassuming. Who knows? Was he indeed born or brought up that way, or did he become inconspicuous later in life — either in response to his war experiences or perhaps as a desperate or feeble survival tool? Maybe unobtrusive inmates had a better chance of "hiding" in the Nazi death camps. I just don't know; he never really spoke to us about his six years of hell on earth.

As Father's Day (and his birthday) approach once

more, I think about this delicate and understated father of mine, and I search for glimpses into his humble, yet loving soul. And I am repeatedly haunted by one most vivid and moving scene from my childhood. But first some contrast.

Several years ago, on a particularly warm Tuesday morning in very late June (yes, June), I found myself walking past a school building in my neighborhood. Lined up in the adjacent street were six idling "coach" buses, brimming with jubilant and frenzied kids. A momentary chill trickled through me. Instantly, one of my fondest childhood memories appeared. Camp departure day had arrived.

Starting at age nine, for 13 years, I had lived and breathed my camping experience — not for two months a year, but for practically every single day of the year. I was obsessed with *everything* about camp. Various scenes from camp visited my dreams all year. (Some still do!) So to say that camp departure day bordered on the euphoric would be a real understatement.

So watching those buses revving up, and listening to those kids howling with glee, was a gripping moment for me. But then it struck me. Something was very wrong with this picture.

It didn't take me long to figure it out. There *was* something missing from the scene. The parents. Where were they?

"HEY!" I shouted internally. "Your children are leaving for camp! Why aren't you here? Can't you at least wait around for the buses to pull out?"

Sweat saturated my collar. I had to find out. I ran to a burly chap with a whistle. He would know.

"Excuse me," I blurted, "I see you're going off to camp."

"Leaving any minute," he offered, crushing a torn duffle bag into the last empty corner of the luggage bin.

"Can I ask you a question?"

"Sure."

"Where are the parents?"

"Oh, a lot of them were here before, but they left. Work, I guess. Who knows? No big deal — these kids are in good hands."

My heart sank. "A lot of them were here," did he say? "No big deal"? Of course it's a big deal. It's the biggest deal of the whole darn year!

It took me a minute or two to fully grasp the reality. I guess the parents *did* have places to go: work, appointments or otherwise. A lot of the kids do have older siblings with them. Why *should* the parents wait for the buses to pull out? Suitable goodbyes, including kisses, nosh and money, are presumably permitted even prior to the buses leaving. And maybe the kids actually prefer to get those mushy goodbyes over with early.

So what got to me?

It was then that I recalled a vivid and moving experience from my own past, on camp departure day.

And it happened every single year, for many years.

My folks woke me early and the three of us made the 80-minute subway trek to the camp bus. Little Jackie (me) didn't get much sleep the night before, dreaming of extra-inning baseball games and stirring Friday night melodies to come. But rest was the last thing on my mind. "The Day" had arrived!

Freshly laundered socks, a chocolate-sprinkle sandwich and my trusted black baseball mitt filled the Korvette's shopping bag I usually carried, and no matter how old I was, Mommy and Daddy had a tough time keeping pace with my determined stride to the "Stairway to Heaven," otherwise known as the camp bus.

Creased loose-leaf papers posed as official bunk signs, directing us to the appropriate lines where we received pre-boarding instructions, obligatory bunk-mate introductions and the usual warnings about throwing stuff out of the bus windows and maintaining proper decorum. But when those big bus doors flew open, we all charged full steam ahead like a herd of police dogs on a manhunt. It's a miracle that other than a lot of crushed Devil Dogs and an exploding Pepsi or two, there were no serious casualties in the mad surge of exuberant youth. I would then make my annual pilgrimage to "the back of the bus" and settle in comfortably at a vacant window seat. Seatmates changed from year to year, but it really didn't matter who was sitting with me. My focus was elsewhere.

Long forgotten by that time were my forlorn father

and mother who, missing me already, remained obediently on the now nearly evacuated sidewalk, chatting with other similarly abandoned parents. I peered out the window and watched them. Sending me to camp was not easy for them. Not financially and not emotionally. Such is the reality for survivors of the Holocaust. Separations cut deep. I was pretty young, and I didn't understand it very well, but I knew it was a real sacrifice.

Before very long, the counselors performed the ritual roll call, and I knew any minute we'd be on our way. I looked once more through the open window and felt that wistful pang of exhilaration and yearning. It was a strange combination of feelings and my stomach knew it. Mommy always wore a look that said, "Everything will be fine," but Daddy looked lost. His lips seemed to quiver, and his soft eyes were no longer dry.

The engines revved up. By now all the windows were crammed with waving arms and blown kisses.

"Bye-bye... See you on Visiting Day... Don't forget to write!"

The wheels began their tiresome thrust. The bus lurched forward. A couple of drops of already opened soda spilled somewhere. And then I heard it. A tap on the windowpane. Strong. Determined. No, maybe frightened is a better word. It was Daddy.

One final goodbye. I saw his hands fumbling in his pockets. When they emerged, they were filled with candy, gum, salted peanuts and some loose change.

He shoved them through the window, half of them spilling to the gutter below. One final chance to feed me, nurture me, hold on to me... love me.

I whipped my neck around to steal a glance at those around me. I guess I was embarrassed, but it didn't matter much. By now Daddy was running to keep up with the departing bus. It was the only time all year he ever ran.

Our eyes met one last time. We were both crying now. His arms flailed in surrender mode as we picked up speed. He knew the separation was inevitable and imminent. It was a race he would surely lose. I stuck my head out for one last look... and stared at the peanuts on my lap. Somehow the bus seemed very quiet.

And so went the annual scene. As I grew older, the candy matured somewhat and the change became dollars. But the loving, tearful face in the window remained the same. It was the happiest sadness I could ever feel.

The irony is that we both knew that Visiting Day would arrive in less than two weeks! It's not like I was going on some yearlong voyage to never-never land. But separations do cut deep.

What really triggered this most reserved man to unabashedly display his most shielded emotions? I don't really know. We never spoke about it. Could it have been a morbid association to the trains he boarded en route to five different concentration camps? Or a menacing reminder of separations —

final ones — that he experienced with loved ones? Or was it some overwhelmingly painful image of the bizarre disparity between the camps he went to, and the camp I loved so much?

I will never know. But I think I now understand why it bothered me so much, when those buses left without parents on that hot Tuesday morning.

And I think I know why I love June so much.

Happy Father's Day, Daddy...and Happy Birthday too... I miss you.

STEPHEN BARON

MY MS ATTITUDE

Overemphasizing the value of having the right attitude is almost impossible. How we present ourselves to the world has a profound effect on how the world treats us in turn. It confirms the old adage, "You reap what you sow."

This has been especially important for me during the last 25 years when I have suffered multiple sclerosis (MS), a progressive, degenerative illness. Interacting with the world and meeting new people while sitting in my wheelchair, I have to decide what kind of person to be. About the last thing I want is to be remembered as a pathetic wretch. Alexis de Tocqueville put it well when he warned that if you present yourself as miserable, you run the risk of

Stephen Baron, age 55, lives in Syracuse and taught political science at SUNY-Oswego.

being despicable as well. So I decided to try the option of kind and loving instead.

I do not think the world owes me anything, and prefer counting all the blessings I have now and have had in the past. Viewed in this way, I've had a blessed life. Is MS a rotten deal? No doubt, but in the great panoply of things that could happen — cancer, car accident, random shooting — MS is not all that bad. MS may make life difficult, but it does not kill.

While I am quadriplegic now, it was not always this way. Rather, it has been a slow progression. I used to swim 500 meters a day and bike many miles at a time. But no more. Over the years, my activity yielded to a leisurely stroll around the block. Progressively, even the walks grew ever shorter and more labored. Finally, I relented and said to my wife, "I think it's time for a wheelchair."

I had always looked upon a wheelchair as a terrible confinement, and vowed never to be in one. I was going to show that stupid illness who's the boss. Tough talk. Was I ever wrong. MS doesn't take to being bossed around. As I have learned, it is in control, and we have to play by its rules.

MS, to explain it medically, is a neurological disorder in which the insulation that protects the nerves (the myelin sheath) is eaten away. The electrical impulses from the brain that make the muscles "fire" are thus prevented from working. Think of an electrical appliance: if the insulation protecting the cord is not there, the appliance short circuits and does not work. A comparable phenomenon occurs with the nerves, hence, paralysis.

Acknowledging the need for a wheelchair indicated that reality had caught up with me. That was 15 years ago.

Part and parcel of being in a wheelchair is having people stare at me. Either silently or aloud, they ask, "I wonder what happened to him?" Young kids stare at me as I hold in my teeth the rubber-tipped stick I use to turn pages. It's so common that I have almost come to expect it. I do not especially enjoy it, but, like so much else, I can't do anything about it. Self-pity is both unflattering and unattractive. Instead, I do my best to make people feel comfortable.

Acceptance was hard won. Denial, contrary to the old joke, is not just a river in Egypt, but also a common theme among MS sufferers.

For more time than I want to admit, I did everything possible to find any sign that I did not have MS. Whenever I exhibited some dexterity or strength, for example, I would say, "See, I don't have MS!" I was really proud of this fiction, and stuck by it vigilantly.

This lasted until the day my feet felt as if they had suddenly grown to size 12 and were trying to fit into my size 7½ shoes. Instantly, my fiction came to a crashing halt. *Oh no*, I said to myself, *I really do have MS.*

Then came the usual wailing and crying. *Why me? Why now? What did I do to deserve this?* Regrettably, it did not change a thing. (It never does.) My wife wasn't about to indulge me in any of this nonsense. As a neurologist and pediatrician, she had seen hundreds of children with painful, terminal conditions. "You had 30 good years!" she scolded in as loving a way as possible. "What about those infants that are destined to die a miserably painful death in a few short years?" What could I say? She was right. Thus ended my reign of self-pity.

Since crying did not help, I turned to my next tried and true solution, cursing. *When all else fails, give 'em a piece of your mind.* And so I did. Whether it was the Maker of the Universe, or my own father, each was subject to my wrath. And of course, this neither changed nor solved anything.

My "bag of tricks" was empty. And I was faced with two choices: first, I could spend all my time being bitter and angry at the rotten hand of cards life had dealt me. But I did not want that. I'd seen the damage it had done to other people.

So that left me with choice number two: to accept that MS would be with me for the long haul, and to try to be the best husband, father, brother, friend, and teacher possible. This is the choice I opted for. Since being diagnosed, I have had a successful marriage (for 24 years and still going), fathered two daughters (born on the same day, two years apart).

For 23 years, I taught political science at the college level, something I took great pleasure in. (I am still in touch with some of my former students by email.) When it got to the point where the students were pushing me to class, feeding me lunch, signing my papers and so forth, I realized that it was time to retire. (Besides, the political correctness in academia was becoming unbearable.)

Acceptance is the crucial first step, but it is only the beginning. What to do with it was still the problem. My days of riding a motorcycle sprang to mind. I recall how a dog would chase me, barking and yelping. I would stop, look it squarely in the eye and say, "Okay, now that you've got it, what are you going to do with it?" 'Twas the same dilemma I faced. Now that I had MS, how was I going to react? Either I could let MS define me, and pursue my life as a victim (become an "MS-er," as one of my neurologists described), or continue life as normally as possible.

So I have relied on reasonable expectations to guide my life. I accept the reality that I am not in any position to have unreasonable expectations, neither of myself, nor of others.

Woe unto the one who does not hold by the policy of reasonable expectations. That person is condemned to a life of frustration over not being able to do the things he once did. As the saying goes, "You can change the future, but you can't change the past."

And then there is the curse of unreasonable expectations of *others*. If we are known for being demanding, who wants to be around us? Sure, considerate family and friends will visit us, but they will eventually tire and come around less and less...until we are left to suffer in loneliness.

156

Being quadriplegic, I have learned what being dependent means. This came as a hard lesson. After all, I have a Ph.D.! When I got my degree, I fully expected the world to be waiting anxiously for the pearls of wisdom to dribble from my lips. Was I ever wrong. Ph.D.s are plentiful, and many drive cabs. And now this.

And I've lowered my expectation of doctors, too. I've learned that M.D. does not stand for Minor Deity, and that doctors cannot "cure" whatever ails us.

Being diagnosed with MS also got me to appreciate how the Almighty controls the world. I have no idea why I got MS. No one does. I just had to accept it as a part of His grand eternal scheme that is beyond my comprehension.

Realizing that God is in control, I am no longer set on changing the world as I once was. Today, my goals are more modest. These days I am occupied writing, corresponding with people all over the world, studying Torah, keeping up with the news, and being the best person I can be. A voice input computer and the Internet have made the first four things possible. The last takes a lifetime of work, and others will judge to what extent I've succeeded.

For me, I'll be satisfied if my children continue to be a credit to my name, and if people will always remember me for the good things I have done.

Finally, I would like to share a poem that I wrote:

I'M TIRED

Of being a quadriplegic
Of always having to sit in my wheelchair
Of needing someone to dress me every day
Of needing someone to feed me every day
Of not being able to sign my name
Of not being able to hold the telephone
Of needing someone to push my wheelchair
Of needing someone to toilet me
Of needing my wife to roll me over in bed
Of not being able to hug my wife or children
But I'm also very grateful for
A loving wife
Two beautiful daughters
A wonderfully supportive extended family
Good friends
Being able to write things that people find interesting
A voice input computer that allows me to write
All things considered, I'm the luckiest man in the world.

GREG YARIS

Do It Now

It was June. I had been working very hard for a number of months, and had just successfully concluded a very large transaction. Physically and emotionally, I needed a break.

An email was pushed to me — a trip to Israel, with speakers I had never heard, and to places I had never been. It was perfect, and my wife graciously agreed. It was fairly last minute and the only flight I could get was Los Angeles to New York to London to Israel. Grueling, but worth it.

The Sunday before my trip, I was barbequing in the backyard and called my father on the cell phone. My parents, who live in Dallas, were going to be in Connecticut for a bar mitzvah the same weekend that

---

Greg Yaris is an attorney living in Los Angeles.

I was flying through JFK, so I thought it would be nice to try and meet.

I was telling my father about the trip, and he was interested in every detail. "Wow, that just sounds wonderful. I wish I could go to Israel again."

And in one of those rare moments of clarity, I blurted out, before I could really think of all the reasons why what I was about to say was wrong, "Why don't you come with me?"

He was stunned. (I was stunned.)

"You are going to be in New York anyway. Just bring two extra shirts and a passport."

My father played his hole card. "The money — it's just too expensive."

It must have been because I was sitting out in the sun, or maybe it was the half a beer I had drunk, but the next thing out of my mouth was, "It's on me. I have a single room and you can stay with me."

Taken aback, my father said, "Let me speak with your mother. I'll get back to you."

Five minutes later, the phone rang. "I'm in."

I gulped. What had been a respite from work had suddenly become a father-son trip. I got online, and ten minutes and one large credit card bill later, he had a seat next to me on the plane and a spot on my trip.

Before I knew it, I was on the way to New York to meet my father. I had mixed emotions — excitement over the trip, but also trepidation about my traveling companion.

160

My father and I were close, but we hadn't lived in the same town for 30 years. Eight days together, without any other family. I couldn't remember ever spending that much time alone with my father.

❖   ❖   ❖

I was waiting by the gate, reading the newspaper, and I felt a hand on my shoulder. I looked up, saw his smiling face, and all trepidation disappeared. With many decisions we make, we can see pros and cons — with this decision, there were only pros.

Two flights and a long cab ride later, we were in Jerusalem. I needed to make phone calls home and to the office. My father (and I'm supposed to be the religious one in the family!) wanted to go to the Western Wall to take pictures. I needed to take a nap; he needed to see the town. Who's the elder one in this relationship?

And it was like that all week. He couldn't get enough. It was like he wanted to take big handfuls of Israel home with him. He couldn't get enough of who we were meeting and what we were seeing. He'd spend each dinner with another table of people from our group. He was the most popular person there.

It's hard to explain how special our time was together. Seeing my father passionate about something so central to who I am, and doing it together, was one of the highlights of my life.

Friday night, we got dressed up and went to the

Wall. And for the first time in my life, I danced to *Lecha Dodi* with my father and a hundred yeshiva boys. And I thought, God willing, maybe my children will take me here someday.

In what really felt like the blink of an eye, we were on a plane back home. Israel, London, New York. At JFK, we parted, him to Dallas, me back to Los Angeles. But when we hugged, we knew that we had done something special together. Something unplanned, unprepared for and, in the end, spectacular.

My father mentioned the trip many times to me over the summer. He sent me copies of his pictures. There we were, in Tel Aviv, overlooking the Mediterranean, smiling together. Memories that will last a lifetime.

In September, my father contracted a staph infection. The doctors didn't know why, and it took weeks of penicillin to cure. He came home older, but determined to recover.

Two weeks after he got home, he was given permission to start exercising. His first morning back on the treadmill, he died, probably of a heart attack.

I miss him badly. I miss him three times a day when I say Kaddish. I miss him in the odd minutes, when I should be working or concentrating on my driving. I'm comforted that he lived a long, fulfilled life, and that although he had much left that he wanted to accomplish, he had accomplished much.

I think back to what might not have been if I hadn't blurted out, "Why not come with me?" If I had stopped to think how much this trip was going to cost. If I had spent even a moment thinking, "Do I really want to burden myself with my father?" One of the greatest opportunities of my life would have been lost.

Sometimes it's better not to think. Sometimes you just have to say, "Do it now." Because if you don't, you may never get the chance.

SARA YOHEVED RIGLER

MY RAT'S TALE

Early one morning, I entered my kitchen and found a persimmon and an apple partly gnawed. Bits of persimmon skin were scattered all over my kitchen counter. Horrified and disgusted, I shrieked for my husband. He called the exterminator.

The exterminator verified that it was a rat, not a mouse. He set three rat traps with chocolate, commenting that rats love chocolate. (A chocoholic myself, I pretended not to hear that I have any affinity with repulsive rodents.)

Sara Yocheved Rigler is a graduate of Brandeis University. Her spiritual journey took her to India and through 15 years of teaching Vedanta philosophy and meditation. Since 1985, she has been practicing Torah Judaism. She is a featured writer on Aish.com, and resides in the Old City of Jerusalem with her husband and children. She is the author of the acclaimed biography/spiritual manual, Holy Woman.

Although I'm always the first one up and the first one to enter the kitchen, the next morning I cowered in our bedroom until my husband went to dispose of the dead rat without my having to see it. Call me a sexist, but it's manifest to me that removing dead rats is a man's job, and all the women I know, even staunch feminists, agree.

Finally my half-asleep, pajama-clad husband dutifully made the rounds of the three traps and reported to me: no rat.

However, another persimmon had been gnawed. And under the dairy sink, I found droppings. The rat had entered the under-sink cabinet from below, through the open space around the drainpipe, and had been feasting on our garbage. I shivered and called the exterminator again.

He moved two of the traps into the cabinet, right next to the drainpipe. The third he left under the refrigerator.

The next morning, as I tried to recite my morning prayers in my room, with my mind on the squished rat under my kitchen sink, my husband again checked and reported: no rat.

"Let's give it another night," my husband suggested. "No rat is that smart."

The next morning, the kitchen was flooded with an inch of water. The rat, apparently thirsty, had gnawed a hole in the plastic tubing to our water filter. The hole was barely two feet away from the shunned trap under the refrigerator.

I called the exterminator again. He was baffled. He had been catching rats for 27 years with those very same chocolate-baited traps. No rat had ever before eluded him.

This time he came with a pump sprayer filled with rat repellent. We knew the rat was living under the cabinet, in the three-inch space between the cabinet and the floor. First the exterminator put a trap right in front of the hole near the wall that the rat had been using to enter that space. Then he started spraying under the sink, right into the circle around the drain-pipe. We waited for the rat to escape out his hole right into the waiting trap.

We waited. And waited. No rat.

Eventually, the exterminator said he had other work to do, and excused himself. My husband went to his Talmud class. I went to my computer, two rooms away, and tried to work. Two hours later, I heard a trap spring.

"Finally," I thought. I waited, cringing by my computer, for my husband to come home and remove the dead rat. When he entered the kitchen, he reported: The trap beside the hole had indeed sprung, but there was no trace of a rat. Somehow the rat had managed to move the trap, thus setting it off, and had scampered to freedom — somewhere else in the house.

For the next two days, there was no sign of the rat. While our nighttime ritual now included locking our fruit bowl in the oven and the ripening tomatoes in the microwave, I decided to leave one persimmon on the kitchen floor, to determine whether the rat was still with us.

The next morning, I found the persimmon, gnawed, on the floor on the far side of the meat counter. At my wits' end, I called the exterminator for the fourth time — a record in his long career of eliminating vermin. While we were loathe to cause suffering to any of God's creatures — even a rat — and had preferred the traps because they killed quickly, now in desperation I told the exterminator to bring poison.

He came armed with two glue traps and three kinds of poison. He found a large hole a few inches away from the gnawed, schlepped persimmon. Clearly, the rat had found a new home beneath the meat counter. It had only one exit. The exterminator put two packets of poison that take three days to work inside the hole. Then he set the two glue traps outside the hole, so that it would be impossible to exit the hole without getting caught. Then he put fast-acting poison powder on the gnawed persimmon, and placed it on the first glue trap, so that the rat, instead of dying a slow and gruesome death from the glue trap, would eat the poisoned persimmon and die quickly. Just for good measure, in case the rat was hiding elsewhere, he put another poisoned persimmon on the other side of the glue traps. It was a comprehensive, foolproof system.

It didn't work. The next morning my husband

reported: No rat, and the persimmons had not been touched.

Incredulous, we stood there staring at our infallible, failed system. Clearly, something uncanny was happening here. Since God runs the world, and all normal means to eliminate this rat had failed, perhaps God was trying to tell us something. But what?

I went to ask Rabbi Mordechai Sheinberger, a kabbalist who lives in our neighborhood. Looking straight at me, he declared: "You need a *tikkun* (spiritual rectification)."

"*Me?*" I asked, chastened. "What *tikkun* do I need?"

"What does the rat say in *Perek Shira*?" Rabbi Sheinberger queried. *Perek Shira* is an ancient poem, attributed to King David, in which every creature and natural phenomenon, from the sky to the desert, from rivers to lightening, from snails to whales, praises God with a particular biblical verse which hints at the essence of that creation.

A friend closely following my rat saga had called me that morning with the startling news: In *Perek Shira*, the rat proclaims, "*Kol haneshama tihallel Yah, Halleluyah*! — The entire soul praises God. Hallelujah!" This is the final, and perhaps most exalted, verse in the Book of Psalms. And it is ascribed to the rat!

I dutifully answered Rabbi Sheinberger: "*Kol haneshama tihallel Yah, Halleluyah!*"

"The *tikkun*," he said with authority, "is to stop complaining."

I stared at him as if he had uncovered a secret vice hidden even from me. *Complain? Me?* I'm no kvetch!

Rabbi Sheinberger continued. "The sages read the verse with slightly different vowels, to mean that with every *breath* you should praise God. Every one of us has received such a wealth of blessings that we should be making a feast of gratitude to God every day. If we don't do that, at the very least we should be praising God with every breath."

I went home, my mind spinning. If I want to get rid of the rat, I need to praise God with every breath and stop complaining? Do I kvetch that much?

That night I removed both glue traps. I left one persimmon laced with the fast-acting poison. In the morning, there was no sign of the rat, and the persimmon was untouched.

As usual, I walked my 9-year-old son partway to school. My son hates this 40-minute walk, which his pediatrician recommends for a variety of reasons. As usual, he stalled, and resisted, and walked at a snail's pace. When my husband returned from synagogue after his morning prayers, I went to greet him with a report about my frustrating morning.

Somewhere between my bedroom and the front door, Rabbi Sheinberger's words flashed through my mind. I realized: This is complaining! I turned my frown into a wide smile, and greeted my husband with an enthusiastic, "Good morning! Isn't it a wonderful morning to be alive? *Kol haneshama tihallel Yah, Halleluyah!*"

Five minutes later I found the rat, dead behind our refrigerator.

❖ ❖ ❖

I did not realize how much I complained. I thought I was simply reporting: my frustrations with the children, how difficult it was to find a parking space, how the new cordless telephone, one week after the warranty expired, stopped working. My newly installed, post-rat complaint radar, however, detected an incessant habit of framing experiences negatively.

I asked myself, *Why? Since how we perceive situations is a choice we make, why would anyone choose misery?*

The answer is part ego, part culture. In television adventure shows, a character's cleverness, resourcefulness and heroism stand out only in relation to the difficulty of the problem he faces. The heroes of *Mission Impossible* were heroes only because their mission was almost impossible.

My ego must have internalized this point early on: If I wanted to be regarded as clever/resourceful/ heroic, I was compelled to emphasize the difficulty of the situation facing me. After all, how would my husband know what an expert mother I am if I didn't apprise him of the childrearing calamities I had to deal with today? How would my friend know what a forbearing and saintly person I am if I didn't tell her the challenges I face from my neighbor?

170

In addition, my cultural indoctrination insists that people who always smile are somehow shallow. Don't they keep up with current events — wars, famines and epidemics? What could they possibly be happy about?

As a college student in the '60s, studying melancholic poets from Baudelaire to T.S. Eliot, I somehow assimilated the notion that people who are depressed are deep. In fact, on our Brandeis campus, if you weren't depressed, there was something wrong with you.

Judaism has a diametrically opposite approach. Many think that the Jewish emphasis on joy dates back to the 18th-century advent of Chassidism. In fact, the Torah itself makes a startling pronouncement. After prophesizing terrible punishments that the Jewish people will have to endure, the Torah proclaims that all this will come upon us "because you did not serve God, your Lord, with joy..." (Deut. 28:47)

Why should the Torah consider the greatest detriment to Divine service to be sadness rather than sin?

Rabbi Shlomo Wolbe explains that the Jewish definition of joy is connection and union, specifically the connection and union of opposites, such as male and female, heaven and earth, Divine and human. If a Jew is connecting to God through the mitzvot, the result, by definition, will be joy. Conversely, if there is no joy, there is no real connection.

Imagine that your beloved surprises you with a getaway to a paradisiacal place. Brightly colored parrots are squawking in the palm trees. A crimson sun is setting into a crystal blue ocean. Your beloved presents you with a bouquet of roses — no, orchids! Then he places before you a basket filled with ripe fruit: pineapples, mangoes, papayas, figs. Sitting atop the fruit is a large box of Belgium chocolates. (Don't forget, this is *my* fantasy!)

Let's say that you sat there morosely complaining because he didn't serve you steak. What does that indicate about the relationship?

But this is precisely the world God has conjured up for us! Sunsets and orchids and daisies and mountains and butterflies and parrots and kittens and mangoes and strawberries and, yes, cocoa beans! Every complaint about what we don't have is a slap in the Divine face, a failure of perception more grievous than any failure of action. If we don't perceive, from moment to moment, how much God loves us and how much He is giving us as an expression of that love, then we are relinquishing the relationship with Him for which purpose, according to Judaism, He created the world.

My post-rat life has a different hue; somber tones have given way to bright splashes of color. Now when people ask me how I am, I reply, "Terrific!" and mean it, without worrying if they'll think I'm shallow or vacuous. I'm not embarrassed to be happy.

Praising God with every breath is a prescription not only against rat infestation, but against every sort of sadness. The process has four steps:

1) Look for the good in the thing or situation

facing you. Set your mind to noticing the *details*.

2) Recognize that everything comes from God, who animates the entire creation — every muscle, neural impulse and atom — at every millisecond.

3) Recognize that God has given this thing or situation specifically to you, because He loves you — individually. Experience the connection.

4) Connection breeds joy. Feel it and thank God!

A contemporary sage recommends the following exercise: Before you eat a fruit, hold the fruit in your hand and contemplate the process God animated in order for you to have that particular fruit. For example, hold a tangerine in your hand, and reflect on how from a tiny tangerine seed, a sapling grew. Over a span of years, God provided lots of sunshine and water so that the sapling would grow into a tree.

Then, last spring, hundreds of flowers — with an intoxicating fragrance — bloomed on the tree. Gradually the flowers fell away and tiny, green fruit emerged. Over a period of eight months, the fruit grew larger and larger. Then it turned a bright orange color.

Then someone picked it, and packed it, and shipped it to the store where you bought it. And God was behind this whole process, just to present you with this tangerine. Then say the blessing, *"Blessed are You, Lord our God, King of the universe, who creates the fruit of the tree."* Then, with your eyes closed, bite into a section of tangerine. Relish its sweetness, its texture, its juiciness, its vitamin C (coming just when you need it in winter), and the way each tiny module of juice is individually packaged. Then relish God's love for you that is expressed in this gift.

After two weeks of practicing this exercise, I'm experiencing what the psalmist meant by, "Taste and see how good is God." Every bunch of grapes has become like the fancy box of candy my husband gives me on our anniversary — a personal expression of tremendous love and caring. The world's greatest joy — the joy of being in a relationship with a loving God — is never further away than my fruit bowl.

MARION LEVY

VICTORIES OF THE HEART

My mother was an astounding woman of great accomplishments. She never went to college. She never earned more than a meager salary. She never dressed fashionably, nor lost the weight she wanted to, despite a lifetime of dieting. She never served as the head of any organization. After marrying my father, she never worked outside the home. All her victories were victories of the heart.

Highly intelligent, my mother graduated as valedictorian of her high school class. She should have

Marion Levy is a pseudonym of a lawyer living in Manhattan. She currently works for a not-for-profit organization which trains minority high school students to qualify for top colleges.

gone to college. She wanted to go to college. But the year before her graduation, her father, Izzy, an immigrant from Poland who owned a dry goods store in Baltimore, suffered a major heart attack. He had to stop working. They sold the store, lived for a year off the proceeds, and waited for their daughter Leah to graduate high school, so she could go to work and support the family.

College could wait, Izzy and Hinda told her. First her younger brother Marvin had to go to college, then medical school, then he would support the family, with a doctor's lucrative salary, much more than any girl — even one with a college degree — could earn.

She did it. She did it happily. She loved her parents. She adored her brother, Marvin. She went to secretarial school, with all the girls who couldn't get into college, and quickly got a job.

Lucky thing she did. A year later the Depression hit. As bread lines formed, my mother brought home her salary, paid in "scrip," not cash, which was used to buy food and necessities — and pay her brother's college tuition. A temporary arrangement. In a few years Marvin would support the family.

Anyway, she would be married by then. In those days, women did not pursue careers for their personal fulfillment. Only women who needed the money worked. She dreamed of getting married, resigning her job, staying home and decorating a living room, and baking *bobka* and cooking blintzes and *kreplach*, just like her mother. She dreamed of having children, pushing baby carriages, knitting little caps and sweaters, just like all her cousins.

❖   ❖   ❖

The Great Depression, however, was a spoiler of dreams. No one could afford to get married. At least not the dutiful, family-oriented Jewish boys that Leah was interested in. They lived at home, worked and handed their whole salary over to Mama, who dispensed it frugally to feed and clothe the entire family, and they stayed single, just like Leah. To get married meant setting up a new household, which entailed buying another stove, icebox, beds, and squeezing a second rental payment out of a skin-and-bones salary. Or it meant, God forbid, to stop contributing to the family coffers altogether, which was unthinkable.

Except to Marvin. Shortly before his medical school graduation, he announced that he was in love, and would be getting married soon. He brought his fiancée home to meet his family.

Margaret was beautiful, with blonde hair and blue eyes. She came from a family of German Jews, three generations in America. They were not at all like us Rabinowitzes. They didn't speak Yiddish, didn't keep kosher, didn't usher in Shabbat with lighting candles and making Kiddush, didn't keep a separate set of Passover dishes and pots in a large barrel in the basement, didn't belong to a synagogue, and didn't drop pennies into a blue-and-white *pushka* in the kitchen, for the sake of purchasing land in Palestine.

Margaret's family was American, and proud of it. Margaret had graduated from Vassar. The Rabinowitzes had never heard of Vassar. Margaret adored the poetry of Yeats. The Rabinowitzes had never heard of Yeats. Margaret dreamed of travel, of culture, of a life of privilege and wealth. For Margaret, Europe meant the Louvre and Venetian canals. For Izzy and Hinda, Europe meant pogroms, from which Hinda had fled at the age of 14, never to see her parents again. Why would any Jew want to go back there?

It is not that Izzy and Hinda did not give their approval to their only son's match. They were never asked.

A month before the wedding, Izzy had a heart attack and died. Leah and her mother were left alone in an apartment in a poor section of Baltimore. Marvin and Margaret bought their first house in a town far away. Leah took a second secretarial job to support herself and her mother.

How did my mother feel about her sister-in-law? Surely she must have felt some resentment at the interloper who usurped her brother's future and diverted his income — which should have supported their widowed mother — into trips to Paris. Surely she must have felt a tinge of regret for the education she had relinquished in Marvin's favor, only to be regarded condescendingly by her pretentious sister-in-law. Surely she must have felt disappointment that

178

she and her mother could not even eat a cooked meal in Marvin's house, for Margaret believed that kashrut was a medieval superstition, a primitive vestige of an outdated religion.

I can only conjecture about the inner battles my mother waged against a battery of natural, destructive emotions. The outcome of the battle, however, was clear even to my juvenile eyes. Who she was, by the time I was old enough to notice, was a woman with no bitterness, no envy, no acrimonious regrets. Moreover, I never in my life heard my mother make any pejorative statement about Aunt Margaret. For me, to whom every petty insult is a *casus belli*, my mother's victory on this front was nothing less than remarkable.

❖ ❖ ❖

Decades later, when my parents, in their old age, moved from their suburban split-level house to an apartment, and I helped them clear out the junk in the basement, I came across a carton of old newspapers, carefully kept. They were a series from the *Philadelphia Inquirer* of 1941. I read them with curiosity, but could not understand why my mother had kept them.

The series started with a front-page Section B letter by a woman named Mary Jones. The letter eloquently, plaintively, described the plight of an apparently vast population of single women who had come of age during the Depression. By the time the

179

Depression ended a decade later, and people could afford to get married, the men in their thirties were marrying women in their twenties. This left the women in their thirties stranded on an island of singlehood, waiting to be rescued, but by whom?

Mary Jones's letter sparked a lively debate. For the succeeding several Sundays, the *Inquirer* printed dozens of responses, supporting or refuting Mary's claim.

I understood why my mother related to this topic. By 1941, she was 31 years old, past the respectable age for a girl to get married. She was pretty, with short black hair and dark eyes, a good conversationalist, had served as the national secretary of Junior Hadassah and was a skilled amateur photographer. She was also — I discovered by asking — Mary Jones.

Not until three long, lonely years later did her cousin Zundel's mother-in-law set up Leah on a blind date with a 40-year-old podiatrist, never married. They met in April and married in August. "He is the most wonderful man in the world," my mother exulted in a letter to her cousin in Palestine, a carbon copy of which she kept for posterity.

In 44 years of marriage, she never changed that opinion.

❖ ❖ ❖

No one had ever told my mother that she should live for herself, so she lived for my father and for us children and for her mother, who became disabled with Parkinson's disease. No one ever told her that domestic work might be drudgery, so she reveled in it, cooking and baking and sewing and embroidering tablecloths that I, her liberated daughter, scorned as a mindless pastime, until she died, and I inherited the precious, every-stitch-laden-with-her-love keepsakes, my most treasured possessions.

My father, it turned out, was the only person who never disappointed her. My sister Susan and I went off and did our own thing, searched, found ourselves far away from home, pursued careers, did not provide her with grandchildren nor call her to ask for recipes for her delicious but cardiologically unhealthy dishes. Her brother Marvin, for whom she had sacrificed college, rarely called, never came to visit, and never contributed to their mother's upkeep. But as for my father — the knight who had rescued her from the workplace and the scourge of singlehood — his armor never tarnished. Even when he was old and arthritic and hard of hearing, the sight of him entering a room lit up my mother's face.

In truth, she got very little of his attention. He worked 12-hour days, six days a week, to support our family, his mother and his mother-in-law, and to send his daughters to expensive private colleges and graduate schools. He would leave the house at 7 a.m., armed with his lunch, lovingly prepared, in a brown bag, and return after 7 p.m., to find his dinner hot on the table. No instant foods, no TV dinners, no cake mixes ever trespassed into my mother's kitchen. She made every dish from scratch, flavored with love.

❦   ❦   ❦

When I was a baby, my maternal grandmother Hinda, whom we called Bubbie, moved in with us. Parkinson's disease, in that era before wonder drugs, left its victims shaking and paranoid. Bubbie needed constant care and could not so much as get up from a chair without help. My mother bathed her, combed her hair, dressed her every morning and undressed her every night. A few times a year, when the Podiatrists' Association had an evening event, my mother would ask me or my sister Susan to take care of Bubbie. We did it, albeit grudgingly, and the next morning would let our mother know that we didn't like the smell of decrepitude in Bubbie's room. Our mother rarely imposed upon us to take care of Bubbie.

When nursing homes became popular repositories for elderly parents, friends kept suggesting to my mother that she find one for Bubbie. My mother would not hear of it. She did not consider her mother a burden. Her love was like a pool of water, making heavy weights buoyant and easy to bear.

When I was 15, Bubbie fell and broke her hip. Now it was impossible to get Bubbie into or out of bed without the muscles of a strong orderly. My mother, defeated, put her into a nursing home and visited every day, for hours, although my grandmother, senile, was long beyond the point of recognizing her daughter.

After just one month in the nursing home, Bubbie died. I, an impudent 15, who did not learn the meaning of filial love until it was too late, thought that after all the years of labor and care, my mother would be relieved. Instead, she was shattered, inconsolable. At the funeral, she could not stop crying, until the rabbi, in his eulogy, mentioned the gallant way my father, throughout the years, had supported his mother-in-law. At that point, my mother told me afterwards, she felt like standing up and applauding.

❖ ❖ ❖

At the age of 58, my Uncle Marvin committed suicide. Aunt Margaret telephoned my brother-in-law, a doctor, and told him that she woke up to find Uncle Marvin dead. On his bedside table were empty bottles of barbiturates. It would be such a disgrace if anyone were to find out! What should she do?

My brother-in-law told her to destroy the empty barbiturate bottles, then to go into her husband's medical office adjacent to their house and find medical samples labeled "Nitroglycerin." She should put these, opened, with some missing, on the bedside table, so it would look like he suffered from a heart condition. Only then should she call an ambulance.

The truth was disclosed by my brother-in-law only to the immediate family.

The after-funeral meal was my mother's finest hour. I felt that as long as Uncle Marvin was gone, there was no more need to be nice to Aunt Margaret. Now my mother could finally tell her off, or at least confront her with the terrible truth of my uncle's suicide.

My mother did no such thing. With all the nobility of her character, she kept Margaret's secret. Margaret, who had turned my mother's only brother against his family. Margaret, whose pretensions to a life of affluence had swallowed up the money which should have been used to support their mother. Margaret, whose unceasing, carping demands had driven Marvin to suicide. Neither in public nor in private did my mother ever excoriate the woman who had ruined her brother's life.

More than that: for every Passover Seder and Rosh Hashana dinner for the rest of her life, my mother insisted on inviting Aunt Margaret, who never had any children. "Why do we have to have Aunt Margaret?" I would complain. "With her stilted accent and her monotonous talk of her stock investments, she ruins every Seder."

My mother's unwavering reply was: "If we don't invite her, she'll be alone on the holiday."

And I, who had infinite compassion for the faceless masses of Biafra and Cambodia, could not stomach my Aunt Margaret, and I could not fathom how my mother could feel such compassion and forgiveness.

❖   ❖   ❖

Somewhere in the middle of my second post-graduate degree, I got it into my head that my mother was an oppressed woman, whose intellect and talents had been stifled, and for what? A husband who never took her out to dinner, and two ungrateful children! I started a campaign to get my mother to enroll in college courses, to earn a degree, to produce something significant with her life.

My mother strenuously resisted my campaign; she knew what her life was about. Although my mother did not articulate it, she believed that the purpose of life was relationship. To her way of thinking, devoting one's life to acquiring anything — money, degrees, status, "professional fulfillment" — was to miss the golden opportunity life provides: to be in relationship. Relationships, my mother felt, provided all that a human being needs in both challenge and fulfillment; succeeding in each relationship was its own unique feat. Becoming a good daughter demanded different skills than becoming a good sister or a good mother or a good wife. Or a good sister-in-law.

When I was 25, I thought my mother had wasted her brains on being just a wife and mother.

Now that I'm 50, I wish I had devoted as much energy to my now defunct marriage as I did to my career.

When I was 25, I thought my mother was a sucker for giving so much to so many while receiving so little in return.

Now that I'm 50, I see that unconditional giving is

Godly, and I wish I had developed in myself such true altruism.

When I was 25, I wanted to be like those who wielded political power.

Now that I'm 50, I wish I was more like my mother, who wielded power over her own impulses and reactions.

When I was 25, I thought I was superior to my old-fashioned mother.

Now that I'm 50, I wish she were alive to read this.

WAYNE KOPPING

KEEPING KOSHER, KICKING AND SCREAMING

For some Jews, keeping kosher is an integral part of their spiritual connection. For me, it just seemed plain weird. I always thought that it would take nothing short of a miracle to convince me it was a viable option. But life sure does have its surprises...

A few years ago, my wife and I moved from Johannesburg to Los Angeles to further our careers in film and television. At the same time, we decided to learn

---

Wayne Kopping is an award-winning filmmaker, currently living in Johannesburg with his wife and kids.

more about our Jewish roots. We found the spirituality and philosophy amazingly powerful.

But *liking* the concepts is a lot different than *living* them. That usually involves some kind of change in one's life — and who likes to change?

The advice we got is to start out slowly. Pick a mitzvah you're comfortable with and then grow gradually.

Great idea. I decided I'd work on "do not murder" for a year or two, and then take it from there.

But my wife, Genevieve, had other ideas. She was already talking about making the kitchen kosher.

"Are you nuts!?" I shrieked. "What will we eat? We'll starve to death!" I tried to appeal to her sense of reason.

But Genevieve is a woman of action. She pulled me into the kitchen and proceeded to pluck cans and bottles off the shelf. To my chagrin, every single item of food in our possession already had a *hechsher*, a kosher symbol. Even my favorite ice cream. We had been practically keeping kosher for months, and I didn't even know it!

I had to concede defeat. Next thing I knew, we had a rabbi in our kitchen blow-torching our oven — kasherizing it, as we called it.

The truth is that keeping a kosher kitchen wasn't even that hard. In fact, I kind of liked it. The real challenge came next: What will I eat at work?

Since I'm always on the move — on location or in a

studio — eating is the least of my concerns. The idea of food becoming a priority in my life was, let's just say, less than appetizing.

Fortunately, I had some flexibility. After all, we were "in transition." So whenever I could, I'd opt to eat at one of the many kosher restaurants around town. But if there weren't any nearby, or if it was really impossible, I'd eat in a non-kosher restaurant, being careful about what I ate.

I was happy to hover "in transition" mode forever — the best of both worlds. Genevieve, however, was leaning toward making more of a commitment. "If God wants me to go 'fully kosher,' " I said half-joking, half-serious, "He's going to have to let me know Himself."

A short time later, two new kosher restaurants opened up right around the corner. I felt an unnerving, cosmic wink.

But that was nothing compared to what came later.

Around the time I was having my strongest existential kosher crisis, a former client called and invited me back to my native South Africa to produce his launch. "You see?" I goaded Genevieve. "How would we keep kosher in Johannesburg? It's just as well we're not 'fully kosher,' or we'd be in trouble."

I set up the production office in my client's building, and didn't give the kosher issue another thought — which was fortunate, since his office served fully catered meals that were naturally not kosher.

A few days later I heard the sad news that they were changing catering companies. And guess who replaced them? A kosher catering company!

It turns out that my client's brother-in-law just happened to own a kosher business that was branching out into catering at that time. This was his first account. So I ate catered kosher meals every day. "Maybe Somebody's trying to tell you something?" Genevieve teased.

I couldn't be sure. But the weirdness didn't stop there. Suddenly, all of Johannesburg seemed to be going kosher! Three new kosher restaurants had just opened up around the city. And to my astonishment, even the studio I edited at had a kosher canteen: an American film crew, with Jewish producers, "just happened" to be in post-production at the time, and they insisted on kosher food.

What was the world coming to?

Even our parents were supportive — they koshered their kitchens for us. But I still managed to convince myself that keeping kosher wasn't a viable option. It was going to take a lot more than a few little coincidences to turn around a hardened cynic like myself.

So I was happy to get back to L.A., where I could bury my head comfortably in the sand.

But there were other plans in store for me...

My younger brother, Allan, came to spend some time with us. He had some business to attend to in San Francisco, so we planned to drive up the coast together.

Throughout my "Jewish Journey," Allan has always been my reality check — constantly quizzing me, pushing me, making sure my feet were planted firmly on the ground. Despite his own deep love for Judaism, he made it his personal mission to make sure I didn't go "too far."

From the moment he got to L.A., he was on the offensive, probing and questioning my motivations. I did my best to explain the serendipitous providence I had been experiencing, and the practical and spiritual benefits of keeping kosher. He still thought I was nuts.

He challenged me for hours on end, all the way to San Francisco. By the time we got there, my head was spinning. I wasn't sure if I'd convinced him, or if he'd convinced me that perhaps I was a *little* overboard.

I knew the kosher thing in San Francisco was going to be tough, so I planned ahead. I armed myself with a list of the local kosher restaurants printed off the Internet.

We checked into our room, and promptly set out to explore the city. Since my brother is a take-charge kind of guy, I let him lead the way — up this street, down the next. I followed as he hopped onto a passing streetcar, and off at some random point.

Finally we ended up in Chinatown. Perusing the stores and restaurants, I realized that I was really hungry, and I was sure Al was, too. I reached for my handy kosher restaurant guide but it wasn't there! I'd inadvertently left it in the room, miles away.

It would take at least 20 minutes to call around and find the closest kosher place — and a whole schlep halfway across town to get there. Surrounded by a thousand restaurants, it all seemed so absurd, and I knew Al wasn't going to be impressed.

Things were about to get ugly.

Is this really all worth it? I wondered to myself. *Does God really care what I stick in my mouth? Maybe it's time for me to be more realistic and forget the whole thing.*

Just then, Al turned to me and asked, "So where are we going to eat?"

I panicked. My eyes darted around, frantically searching for an Internet café. It was hopeless. I didn't want to get into another confrontation with my brother.

I was about to give in, when another voice inside me yelled, "You wimp! You're going to give up that easily?! Stand up for what you believe in!"

That was it. I just had to do the right thing.

I was about to tell Al to brace himself for a 45-minute delay, when out of the corner of my eye I noticed something strangely out of place: Hebrew writing. I looked again closely and spelled out the words, "G-l-a-t-t K-o-sh... Glatt Kosher!"

Right there, smack in the middle of Chinatown — a kosher restaurant!

I couldn't believe it.

And neither could Al.

There were no more questions. My most ardent

challenger had unwittingly led me through the streets of San Francisco, only to find the answers we both were looking for.

From then on, keeping kosher was no longer an issue for me.

And it solidified a basic rule of life: When you set out to do the right thing, the Universe conspires to make it just a little bit easier.

SARAH SHAPIRO

WHEN MOMMY STOPPED DRIVING

When the doctor delivered the news, we were abashed and afraid. How much time did we have?

When she started to walk haltingly, we were abashed and afraid. She'd never moved around slowly like that before in her life!

When the lab test came back, we were so relieved. It looked like she was going to make it! When she got

Sarah Shapiro is the author of Growing with My Children; Don't You Know It's a Perfect World?; and A Gift Passed Along (ArtScroll). She is the editor of the Our Lives anthologies, most recently The Mother in Our Lives (Targum). She writes regularly for various publications, and teaches writing and speaks on a variety of topics in Israel and the United States.

some of her energy back, we were so happy!

When she started to sit down a lot, we were abashed and afraid.

When she stopped reading everything except the morning paper, we were abashed and afraid. She had always been such a big reader.

When she stopped driving, we were abashed and afraid. She had always driven everywhere!

Now she sat in the passenger's seat.

When she stopped reading the morning paper and we'd read to her, we longed to see her with *The New York Times* in hand.

It took her forever just to make herself breakfast.

When she started lying down right after breakfast, we got worried. We wished she would spend her mornings sitting up.

When she'd drop off to sleep while being read to, we wished she'd listen all the way through.

When she could no longer stand there to make breakfast, we were abashed and afraid. She was the one who always fed everybody! She had always made herself breakfast! We couldn't believe what was happening. We made her breakfast.

When she could only eat half, we longed to see her finishing everything on her plate, the way her father had taught her; all her life she'd obeyed him.

We longed to see her in the passenger's seat.

When she didn't have the energy to listen, we looked back wistfully at the way we used to read to her, and wished we had read to her more. We could have read her various things. Why hadn't we taken her places? Maybe she would have enjoyed the museum.

We longed to see her in her chair.

When she couldn't get out of bed, we thought: *Just yesterday she got out of bed!* It seemed so long ago. She'd walk across the living room to the kitchen.

When she couldn't feed herself anymore, we fed her, shyly.

When she could only finish about a third, we yearned for the time when she'd eat half.

When we realized she couldn't swallow, we thought to ourselves: *Just yesterday she was able to eat.*

When she stopped speaking, we looked back on our little conversations as if they were diamonds.

We sit and watch. She doesn't seem to be seeing us.

But she is breathing!

We rejoice. She is breathing!

MICHELE THALER

JUST DOING

This past Shabbat, with my husband away in England for work, I had a friend come over and stay for three days with her three children because *her* husband was away in New York. Another friend of ours who had a baby not long ago wanted to "get away," so she too came for Shabbat with her husband and two children. In addition, there was a young woman who stayed with us to help with the children, another young woman who recently gave birth with her new baby, my mother-in-law, and my own seven children.

It was quite a houseful, with four babies under

Michele Thaler grew up in Philadelphia. She's been in Israel for 20 years, and lives in Jerusalem with her husband, children, mother-in-law and a cast of extras. She does counseling privately and is the director of peer counseling at Israel's only Center for Independent Living.

seven months old, two toddlers, and three more under age five. Just the logistics of who would sleep where and with whom, who would sit where at the table, and who needed a bottle, nursing or a diaper change might have been enough to turn the heart of the bravest army general, however well-schooled in the art of combat control.

That was this week.

Last week, I had a different friend come with two small children. She stayed for four days, while her husband took their older children on their yearly visit to grandparents in Florida. Thursday morning, when I was just beginning to contemplate my Shabbat preparations, my downstairs neighbor came in. (His wife was in New York, visiting her ailing father.)

"Michele, how do you cook a chicken?"

"Don't worry, Shmuel, just bring it to me and I'll be glad to cook it for you. But you can't just make one chicken. You have eight children to feed."

"That's okay; we'll fill up on soup."

"Fine, bring me a chicken."

"Um, Michele, I really don't have any ulterior motives, but can I just ask you one more question?"

"Sure, Shmuel, go ahead."

"How do you make soup?"

"Oh forget it. Just come for Friday night dinner. You'll have to bring me an extra table and some silverware, though, okay?"

We both laughed, and that Friday night, we were

seven adults and 17 children. Somehow we even managed to squeeze in three high-chairs and an infant seat around the table.

My friends are always asking me: How do you do it? How do you manage? And some of you may be thinking, "Is she crazy? It's all I can do to get supper on the table for my family!" while others may be thinking, "What's the big deal? A few Shabbat guests? We do that and more every week."

So what *is* the big deal anyway? I am doing all this cooking, preparing, planning, entertaining, and cleaning up while sitting in a wheelchair.

Four years ago, during the routine delivery of my fifth child, my doctor (with my consent) called for an anesthesiologist to administer an epidural anesthetic. The epidural caused bleeding into the spinal column, and because of the neglect of the doctor and hospital staff, I remain a paraplegic to this day.

I can't begin to convey the upheaval this caused in my family and my life. Instead of spending two days in the hospital followed by a few days in a mother-and-baby convalescent home, and then coming home in time for the bris, I spent three days lying in a hospital bed not knowing what had happened to me. Then I was whisked by ambulance in the middle of the night to a second hospital for an operation that the surgeons warned me might not help, because it was "already too late."

At the urging of my surgeon, I made it to the baby's bris. I arrived in an ambulance, looking surprisingly well, considering what I had gone through that week.

I didn't actually make it home to stay for almost six months, during which time I was in the rehab unit of Hadassah Hospital where I received physical therapy, occupational therapy, and scores of lessons in life from the nursing staff and fellow patients. It would be impossible to make an accounting of the hours I spent with therapists, social workers, nurses, interior designers and builders, as well as family, friends and fellow patients, discussing and planning how my life would unfold once I was again at home and with my family.

"The kitchen has to work for me. I do a lot of cooking and entertaining."

"The living room has to be open and spacious. We host a lot of Torah classes in the house and we like to have Shabbat guests."

"I'm still the Mommy, I have to be able to bathe my kids, feed them, and sit with them to do homework."

"We have to have a place for a crib. When we have more children, God willing, I'll have to have them near me."

"*More children?!*" The doctors and nurses were incredulous when my husband and I asked them how my condition would affect future pregnancies and births.

"*More children?!*" Even my interior designer, a close friend and the wife of a great Torah scholar, was shocked by the thought. "I couldn't take you seriously when you talked about more children," she told me recently. "But I didn't want to sound discouraging, so I went along with it. Now look at you, two more children and you're doing great!"

"*Doing great.*" I actually hear that a lot. I hear it from my friends, my husband and people who knew me back then.

"*Doing great.*" What does that mean? Does it mean that I am managing it all without any help? No, I actually have plenty of help: babysitters, and housecleaners and an army of high school girls who march in and out of my house for the two hours of community service (*chesed*) they do each week.

Does it mean that I never get upset or frustrated at my disability? No, there are many things that I find frustrating and upsetting: the fact that I miss more celebrations than I attend because the halls are inaccessible or the elevator is not operating; the fact that I can rarely complete a task in the house without calling for help — to get something out of reach or to pick up something I've dropped; the times I've been stuck in the bathroom because someone left my bedroom door open, giving anyone in the hall a clear view of me exiting the shower; the times I've been stuck in my bed because I didn't have clothing to wear and no one was at home to help; the time my wheelchair was stuck with a broken axle or a flat tire; the times I've been left sitting in the chair in the street or parking lot, tears of frustration coursing down my

201

cheeks because the building I was assured had wheelchair accessibility didn't; the times I've been left alone in the house, a baby happily playing on the floor, only to have him begin to wail the moment there was no one else there to pick him up.

I could go on and on, but there wouldn't be any point. And this certainly isn't my point.

So what do my friends, family, husband and neighbors all mean when they shake their heads and say, "You're doing great"? I guess it could mean that I joyfully accept what the Almighty has given me, knowing that in His infinite wisdom He has chosen this path for me.

I guess it could also mean that instead of wallowing in my circumstances, I have chosen to go on with my life full speed ahead, having more children, Shabbat guests, *chesed* projects, and more.

It could mean that I've worked on myself throughout this test and came out of it a better person in some ways than when I went in.

But I don't think about it this way. I don't sit and wonder whether I am doing great or not so great. I'm too busy living my life, raising my kids, cooking my meals, writing my stories, acting in plays, making my friends.

If you ask me, I'm not doing great. I'm just doing.

MALKA WINNER

HER NAME WAS PATIENCE

er name was Patience, and that was enough to do her in. But there was more: Patience lived in the poorer part of town with broken-down cars and other junk in her yard, and her house was the last stop for the school bus, so everyone on the bus saw the undesirable conditions in which she lived. She was doomed.

Maybe there would have been more hope if her name had been normal — like Katie or Anna. But Patience was unusual — in name and life — and the kids knew it.

Malka Winner is a wife, mother and freelance writer and editor residing in Jerusalem, Israel.

Every morning went like this: all the kids would get on the bus, chatting away, looking out the window, doing what kids do. And then the bus would turn onto the main road of our small Massachusetts town and head for school, making one last stop — at Patience's house.

As the bus door creaked open, there would be silence as the kids watched Patience climb in. She didn't really stand out in a crowd, but the kids had decided that she did. Her clothes weren't as nice, her hair was limper, and, like dogs that smell fear, my class-mates sensed her terror.

As she made her way down the aisle looking for a seat, someone would inevitably yell, "Patience, have patience!" and then the kids would all scream, "Patience, Patience, Patience!" And she would walk up and down the aisle of the bus to cries of "Patience! Patience!" looking for a seat, only to be repeatedly refused with, "Can't sit here" and "Seat's taken."

The kids would even spread themselves out in their seats, manipulating their belongings to take up as much room as possible, because no one, absolutely no one, wanted to be the one to sit with Patience. And if Patience would sit beside you, you'd have "the cooties" for at least a day, possibly even two or three.

And so it went, day in and day out. Patience would get on the bus, the kids would scream her name, tease her, and refuse to let her sit with them. Patience would inevitably force her way into a seat as the bus driver yelled at her to sit down already, always oblivious to her situation, and the unlucky seat partner would cringe and scoot as close to the window as possible, to avoid contamination.

Patience never cried. She never attempted to defend herself. She never made eye contact. She just looked straight ahead and walked from seat to seat, back and forth, until she had a place to sit, and then got off the bus and disappeared into the school building, knowing that she would have to face the same thing tomorrow morning. It had to be excruciating.

And every morning when I would get on the bus, I would try to figure out how I could avoid being the one with whom Patience decided to sit. I would scan the seats for one with somebody already in it, and if none were available, I'd sit in an empty one, hunker down, and begin to pray. I'd pray that Patience wouldn't sit with me. I'd pray that she'd sit somewhere else. I'd pray that if she did sit with me, that I wouldn't become the object of teasing and torment. These things worked by association, you know.

And when she did sit with me, which to my dismay happened with a certain degree of frequency, I would turn, face the window, and pretend to be very interested in the passing scenery. But every so often, when I was sure she wasn't looking, I would cast a furtive glance at her, peeking at the face that had endured so much. And like always, she would be staring straight ahead, with a blank, unreadable and distant expression on her face. And I would find myself flooded with guilt.

205

I am ashamed to admit that this teasing went on for years. And the most I could do was feel guilty. Quite simply: I was a coward, and I was terrified that if it wouldn't be her, it would be me.

It has been something like 15 years since I rode that bus every morning, avoiding Patience, secretly feeling terribly guilty and sorry, and trying to glimpse the personality inside the abused shell. And I have thought of her almost every morning since.

Looking back, I don't blame myself for my cowardice. Children can be the cruelest of tormentors. Their actions and words toward one another can cause serious damage. I was terrified of being the next victim. But now I can't help but wonder what would have happened if I'd invited her to sit with me, or if I'd made room for her in my seat as soon as she came on the bus. I never screamed her name, and I never told her she couldn't sit with me, but I passively participated by not extending myself. I never did anything, but then again, I never did anything.

Sometimes I wonder what happened to Patience. What kind of person did she become? What kind of person could she become, after so many years of torment? What happens to a child who daily has her every vestige of self-esteem and dignity torn from her? These thoughts turn my stomach. And I realize that I have never forgiven myself.

And I wonder why I never prayed for her those mornings on the bus. At least if I wasn't going to defend her or invite her to sit with me, I could have prayed that the teasing would stop. Instead, I prayed only for myself.

I did not pray for her then, but I can pray now. I pray that no person, anywhere, in any circumstances, should ever be the object of baseless hatred. I pray that children will be nice to each other and learn that "the cooties" aren't real. And I pray that I can teach my children that passively sitting by only perpetrates the problem, and that treating others with dignity, no matter how difficult, is what counts. And I pray that I can give them the confidence to do this.

The time has finally come to ask Patience for forgiveness. I don't know where she is or what she looks like now, but I sense that there is some of her in all of us, a little part of us that has faced some abuse, suffered some injustice, and holds some grudge. Please let go, move on. Please don't let there be any more victims. Don't let there be any more perpetrators. Give respect and honor where it's due. And... please forgive me.